How Far to Follow?
The Martyrs of Atlas

Bernardo Olivera

ST. BEDE'S PUBLICATIONS
Petersham, Massachusetts

Saint Bede's Publications
P.O. Box 545
Petersham, MA 01366-0545

Cover photograph courtesy of the archives of St. Joseph's Abbey, Spencer, Massachusetts. Photographs facing page 5 courtesy of the Trappist Generalate, Rome, Italy.

Initials and some names have been changed in order to protect the identity of those involved in the events related in this book.

LIBRARY OF CONGRESS CATALOGING-IN-PUBLICATION DATA
   Olivera, Bernardo.
      How far to follow? : the martyrs of Atlas / by Bernardo Olivera.
      p. cm.
      ISBN 1-879007-24-X (pbk.)
      1. Trappists--Algeria--Tibehirine--Biography. 2. Christian martyrs--Algeria--Tibehirine--Biography. 3. Victims of terrorism--Algeria--Biography. 4. Notre Dame de l'Atlas (Monastery : Tibehirine, Algeria) 5. Tibehirine (Algeria)--Church history--20th century. I. Title.
      BX4155.O45 1997
      272'.9'0965--dc21   97-4714
                                                              CIP

Contents

Fr. Christian

Fr. Christopher

Br. Luke

The Trappist Martyrs
of Atlas
May 21, 1996

Fr. Celestine

Fr. Bruno

Br. Michael

Br. Paul

Preface

Our Seven Witnesses

It is impossible to forget it. We cannot simply turn the page and continue our life as if nothing had happened. They did not die in vain. Christ loved the Algerian people so much that he gave his life for them. Our brothers, too, who followed Jesus so closely, have given their lives. We have good Easter memories and it is precisely in the Easter mystery that our aching heart meets these beloved faces again.

With words like these Brother Christian referred to the many martyrs who had gone before him in the road of the total gift of self. He was speaking towards the end of 1995. Today his words become ours when we speak about him and his six companions, all from the same community, all innocent victims of terrorism. Our brothers of Atlas are no longer among us. They went before us and wait for us, so that we can all enter together, like good cenobites, into the kingdom of God.

The substance of this book is made up of four letters written soon after the events took place, letters which express my faith, love, contemplation and grief over what happened. I share them with you to keep the memory of our witnesses alive, to make known the wonders which God worked in their lives and to renew our hope for a peace which is longed for, yet seems so far away. The letters also call attention to the Spirit's work in the suffering, joyful, faithful Church in Algeria. In the final analysis, I share them with you because a light which shines so strongly cannot be hidden under a bushel basket. It is set on a lampstand, where it gives light to all in the house.

The seven brothers were kidnapped on March 27 and beheaded on May 21, 1996. They were all French and had received their monastic formation in different monasteries in France: Bellefontaine, Aiguebelle and Tamié.

Dom Christian de Chergé was born on January 18, 1937 at Colmar in the province of Haut-Rhin. He entered the monastery of Atlas on August 20, 1969, as a priest of the Archdiocese of Paris, having been ordained on March 21, 1964. He made his novitiate with the community of Aiguebelle, but his solemn profession was at Atlas on October 1, 1976. He had studied in Rome from 1972 to 1974 and was deeply involved in interreligious dialogue. In fact he was the inspiring spirit of the Islamic-Christian dialogue group known as *Ribat es Salam* (Bond of Peace). He was elected Titular Prior of Atlas in 1984, which is the year when I first met him, on the occasion of the Trappist General Chapter held at Holyoke, Massachusetts. We were both new superiors without much experience and this common condition created a bond between us from the very first day we met. After my election as Abbot General he called me, "My father and my brother." Three weeks before being kidnapped he preached a retreat during which he left the following recommendation:

> "Thou shalt not kill": not kill yourself, not kill time (which belongs to God), not kill trust, not kill death itself (by trivializing it), not kill the country, the other person or the Church. There are five pillars of peace: patience, poverty, presence, prayer and pardon.

Brother Luke Dochier, the oldest member of the community, was born on January 31, 1914 at Bourg-le-Péage, in the province of Drôme. He entered the monastery of Aiguebelle on December 7, 1941, arrived at Atlas in 1946 and made solemn profession on August 15, 1949. He thus lived over half a century in Algeria and was very well known in the whole region for his untiring medical assistance to those who came to the monastery. Within the community his special contribution was his mixture of good humor and solemn wisdom, together with his skill as a cook. He was a laybrother by vocation and at heart. I still remember his question to me, "What has happened to the laybrothers?" He rarely showed the treasure hidden in his heart, but when he entered the select "club of eighty" he told the brothers in their meeting room.

Tibhirine has withstood both the war and the terrorists.... It is a mystery. When I am dying, if it is not a violent death, I would ask that you read me the parable of the prodigal son and say the Jesus Prayer. Then give me a glass of champagne, if there is any, so that I can say good-bye to this world...before drinking the new Wine (Christopher's *Journal*, Jan. 30, 1994).

Father Christopher Lebreton was born on October 11, 1950 in Blois, province of Loir-et-Cher. He entered the monastery of Tamié on November 1, 1974, and made solemn profession there on the same day in 1980. He transferred to Atlas in 1987, was ordained priest on New Year's Day 1990, then named novice master and subprior. He was an untiring writer, an enthusiastic guitar player, a poet at heart, always on the side of the poor and the outcast. Our first meeting was on the landing of the guest house staircase at Tamié, on December 18, 1990. Christopher was coming down two steps at a time and I was slowly going up in the dark. We met with a bang! He had an uncommon gift for Christian friendship and in his first letter to me wrote:

Something has remained after your visit. I am simply sure that Jesus, our common brother, has brought the two of us together.

Brother Michael Fleury was born on May 21, 1944 at Sainte Anne in the province of Loire Atlantique. He had been a member of the Institute of Prado and had lived for some ten years in Marseille in close contact with the Muslim immigrants from North Africa. He entered the monastery of Bellefontaine on November 4, 1980, transferred to Atlas in 1984 and made solemn profession there on August 28, 1986. He was a man of few words, a silent hard worker. He would always repeat, "*Inch Allah!* God protect you!" That is how he said good-bye to me several years ago after I had visited the community. He offered his life for Algeria and his offering was consummated on his fifty-second birthday.

Father Bruno Lemarchand was born March 1, 1930 at Saint Maixent in the province of Deux Sèvres. The years of his early childhood were passed in Algeria where his father was stationed as a soldier. Before becoming a monk he was the superior of an important preparatory school and priest of the Diocese of Poitiers, ordained April 2, 1956. He entered the monastery of Bellefontaine on March 1, 1981, transferred to Atlas in 1989 and pronounced his solemn vows on March 21, 1990. Two years later he was named superior of Atlas's annex house at Fes in Morocco. He was at Atlas when the kidnapping occurred because he was planning to assist at the election of the titular prior there, which was scheduled for March 31, 1996. He was a man of great discretion and simplicity, and had prepared for monastic profession with these words which reveal his inner heart:

Here I am before you, my God…. Here I am, rich in misery and poverty, full of unspeakable cowardice. Here I am before You, who are nothing but Mercy and Love.

Father Celestine Ringeard was born on July 27, 1933 at Touvois, the same province as Brother Michael, Loire Atlantique. He was marked for the rest of his life by his military service in Algeria. After his ordination as a priest for the diocese of Nantes, on December 17, 1960, he exercised his pastoral ministry with the dropouts, prostitutes and homosexuals of that city. He entered Bellefontaine on July 19, 1983, transferred to Atlas in 1987 and pronounced his solemn vows on May 1, 1989. He was especially gifted with sensitivity, compassion and easy interpersonal relations. I do not remember ever having met any monk with such a capacity for verbal communication. He loved music and was the community's organist and cantor. After the first visit of the Armed Islamic Group (GIA) on Christmas Eve 1993, he had to undergo an extremely delicate heart operation.

Brother Paul Favre Miville was born on April 17, 1939 at Vinzier, Haute-Savoie. He worked as a professional plumber, then entered the monastery of Tamié on August 20, 1984. After transferring to Atlas in 1989, he made solemn profession on the same day seven years later, August 20, 1991. He was skilled in all types of manual work and was responsible for the irrigation system in the monastery's garden. He returned from a trip to France on March 26 only a few hours before the kidnapping took place. It is clear that he had a date with the GIA and with...divine Providence. On January 11, 1995 he had written:

> How far can you go to save yourself without running the risk of losing true life: only one Person knows the day and the hour of our liberation in him.... We should be open to his action in our lives by prayer and loving presence to all our brothers.

These are our seven brothers. They formed a group like many others we can meet in our monasteries or parishes, or on the streets of our cities. Some were withdrawn, others communicative. Some were placid, others highly emotional. Some were more inclined to intellectual work, others to manual work. What united them was their search for God in community, their love for the Algerian people and a bond of unbreakable fidelity with the pilgrim Church in Algeria.

Their daily contact with the voice of the Spirit through sacred reading always helped them to discern the hand of God in the events they lived through. Some of the Lord's words echoed with intense clarity in the ear of their heart. Jesus says, "Whoever serves me must follow me, and where I am, there also will my servant be." Our seven brothers understood it well—to serve Jesus means to help him where he is. Where and when is that? It is in the *hour* of the supreme struggle on Calvary, when he and we are on the cross! For this there is no need to be a hero. Quite the contrary! They knew very well that our strength lies in our weakness, which in turn relies on God.

> The word, "martyr," is so ambiguous in our context!… If something happens to us, although I do not wish it to, we want to live it here in solidarity with all the Algerians, men and women, who have already paid with their lives, and in union with all unknown innocent victims… It seems to me that He who is helping us to continue on today is the One who has called us here. I am continually amazed at it all (Michael, May 1994).

Jesus, the Teacher, says:

> You have heard that it was said, "You shall love your neighbor and hate your enemy." But I say to you, love your enemies, and pray for those who persecute you, that you may be…perfect, just as your heavenly Father is perfect (Mt 5:43-48).

It was only because they were following Jesus and entering with him into the tender mercy of the Father, that our seven monks wanted to live a brotherhood that went to the limits which it did. This is why they used to speak of "our brothers of the mountains and our brothers of the plains" to refer to the armed terrorists and the armed military who fought in their area. This is also why we can believe that, when their hour had come, they were given enough spiritual clarity to ask forgiveness from God and from their human brothers, just as they themselves forgave from their hearts those for whom they, like Jesus, were laying down their lives.

"Where I am, there also will my servant be" (Jn 12:26). Where is that? The truth is that it will be on Calvary and on the cross—only, however, as a step in the paschal mystery toward the Father, because Jesus says, "The Father will honor whoever serves me," and adds:

> I am the way and the truth and the life. No one comes to the Father except though me…. I am in the Father and the Father is in me (Jn 14:6-10).

On the feast of St. Joseph, 1996, Christopher gave what would be his last homily on this earth. At the end he exclaimed:

> May we let Joseph go! May we let Jesus come to us! In the life of Jesus, as man, there is something of Joseph's energy, just as there is, of course, something of the attractiveness of Mary, his mother. It is the inheritance transmitted from Abraham. But Jesus himself is leaving. And he knows where he is going, where he is taking us: "I am going to the Father."

It is perhaps during these last days that our brother Christopher, sensing what was coming, raised his hands and offered this prayer that bursts from his heart:

Let's go, Father,	*let's go say thanks*
	let's go to Christ
Let's go, Father,	*let's go as Church*

> *let's go in Faith*
> *let's go in Wind*   *to say I love you*
> *let's go for peace and true bread*
> *and for freedom*   *it is time to finish*
>   *with the Evil one*
>   *by a kiss from you*
>   *to make all new*
>   *and beautiful*
>   *in Love*
> *Let's go from here, brothers, a sacrifice of praise*
>   *to God*

Three years ago—it was March 1994—I met Christian in the French monastery of Timadeuc. I told him, "The order does not need martyrs. It needs monks." He listened to me and did not reply. Then he looked at me and said, "There is no contradiction." Today I see that he was right: monks and martyrs. The order, the Church, the world, we all need faithful witnesses who speak words of blood from the inexhaustible fountain of their first love. We need followers of Jesus who are ready to follow him to the end, eager to embrace the cross of forgiveness that gives freedom and salvation. God has given us all of this in the persons of our brothers.

Our seven martyrs speak very specially today to the Church in Algeria and to other local Churches that suffer for being faithful to the Gospel:

> The first and the last, who once died but came to life, says this:
> —and they say it with him—
> "I know your tribulation and poverty, but you are rich" in faithful and true witnesses.
> "Remain faithful until death, and I will give you the crown of life" (Rev 2:8-11).

This small Algerian Church, that has chosen "shared weakness as the language of God Incarnate," has a mystery to reveal and to communicate to the whole universal Church. "Whoever has ears ought to hear what the Spirit says to the Churches:"

Where, death, is your victory? Life has overcome death through the love which the Father has for us in Christ Jesus our Lord!

Rome, Jan. 8, 1997
Bernardo Olivera, Abbot General OCSO

CHAPTER I
The Initial Facts
A Faithful Reading of the Events

May 27, 1996

Very dear Brothers and Sisters,

In these days immediately following the assassination of our seven brothers of Atlas, it seems important to try to reread in the light of faith the events which have affected us all so deeply ever since we heard the announcement.

A Lasting Testimony

The Apostolic Letter *Tertio Millennio Adveniente* (TMA) of Pope John Paul II concerning preparation for the Jubilee of the Year 2000 recalls that the Church of the first millennium was born from the blood of martyrs. *This is a testimony not to be forgotten*, he writes. (TMA, 37) Our brother monks of Atlas leave us this same testimony today, when we are about to celebrate in 1998 the nine hundred years of the foundation of Cîteaux and, two years later, the 2000 years since the birth and death of Jesus Christ. We cannot let their testimony be forgotten!

The mystery of the human person, of every person, is only truly manifest in the mystery of the Word made flesh: the Word made human. The testimony of our brothers, like that of all of us as monks and nuns, or as believing Christians, can only be understood in the light of the testimony of Jesus Christ. And here is the testimony of the Faithful Witness: God is Love! Father, forgive them for they do not know what they are doing! Your kingdom come! Forgive us our sins as we forgive those who have sinned against us!

1
Stability until Death

Communities of the Order and Stability

The decision made by the brothers of Atlas is not unique. All of who belong to the Benedictine-Cistercian tradition have taken a vow of stability. It binds us until death to our community and to the place where that community lives. Many communities of our order faced with war and armed violence in the course of these past years have had to reflect seriously on the meaning of this vow and make the crucial decision as to whether they should stay where they are or leave. This was the case with the communities of Huambo and Bela Vista in Angola, with that of Butende in Uganda, with the community of Marija Zvijezda at Banja Luka in Bosnia, and quite recently with our brothers of Mokoto in Zaïre. While Huambo, Bela Vista, Butende and Marija Zvijezda chose to remain where their monastery was, the community of Mokoto decided to take the road to exile. In each of these cases the decision was taken by the whole community after prolonged reflection and discussion.

How can we understand the depth of this vow in the life of a monk or nun? Perhaps the text of a letter of Father Christian can help us understand better the meaning of our vow. He had planned to send it on December 28, 1993 to Sayah Attiya, chief of the Armed Islamic Group (GIA) and head of those who came to the monastery that Christmas Eve.

> Brother, allow me to address you like this, as man to man, believer to believer.... In the present conflict in which our country is engaged it seems impossible for us to take sides. The fact that we are foreigners forbids it. Our state as monks (*ruhbân*) binds us to the choice God has made for us, which is a life of prayer, simplicity, manual work, hospitality and sharing with everyone, especially with the poor.... These essential qualities of our life have been chosen freely by each one of us. They bind us until death. I do not think that it is the will of God that this death should come to us through you.... If one day the Algerians state that we are not welcome, we will respect their desire to see us leave, although we would regret it deeply. I know that we will continue to love them ALL, and that includes you as one of them. When and how will this message reach you? It doesn't matter! I needed to write it to you today. Forgive me for having done it in my mother tongue. You will understand me. And may the ONE Creator of all life lead us! AMIN!"

Community Discernment

I think it is important to recall here the major stages of the discernment made by the community of Atlas after the visit of six armed persons on Christmas Eve, 1993. The latter had sought to compromise the monks and force them to collaborate with the armed movement by giving it medical aid, economic support and logistical help. When the Prefect, or *Wali*, of Medea offered the monks armed guards, the brothers refused on the grounds that they wished to be a sign of peace for everyone. For the same reason they refused to live in the "protected" area of Medea rather than in the monastery. They did, however, agree to close the monastery doors from 5:30 P.M. to 7:30 A.M. and to have a new telephone line laid to the house of the gatekeeper.

In the days that followed the visit of Christmas Eve, the monks decided, through a series of community votes, to reject any form of collaboration with the armed group except medical attention in the monastery itself, if needed. They also decided to remain in Atlas, though provisionally reducing the number of brothers in the monastery. This meant not returning to France if they had to leave Atlas someday, but rather to go to Morocco and wait there until circumstances enabled them to return to Atlas. Finally they made the decision not to receive any novices at Atlas.

The apostolic nuncio had invited them, in a letter of June 24, to come and live at the nunciature in Algiers. To this the brothers replied that for the moment they did not see the need to transfer the community to the nuncio's residence, but if the time came for this, they would discern with the nuncio and the bishop what they ought to do.

On December 16, 1994, at the end of further community discussions, the brothers took new votes and confirmed their option of the previous year. Archbishop Teissier, who had come to visit them during this time, left them a message in which he thanked them for taking the risk of prolonging their presence and their witness to Christ, even though armed groups were passing through their district with increasing frequency. He told them again how significant their presence of prayer and daily work in Tibhirine was for the whole Christian community of Algeria and he thanked them for their courageous fidelity.

The Possibility of Violent Death

In the discernment which led to the decision to remain at Atlas despite the tense situation surrounding them, the monks were aware of the possibility of a violent death. The letter Father Christian wrote me after the assassination of two religious sisters in September 1995 said it clearly:

> The memorial celebration had a beautiful atmosphere of serenity and self-offering. It brought together a very small church, whose remaining members are completely aware that from now on their presence must logically include the possibility of a violent death. For many it is like a new, radical immersion into the charism of their congregation…and a return to the source of their first calling. At the same time it is clear that the desire of us all is that none of these Algerians, to whom our consecration binds us in the name of the love which God has for them, would wound this love by killing any of us or any of our brothers.

Father Christian's thoughts on the possibility of a violent death had become his prayer, that of a man who wants to be totally disarmed of any form of violence when facing his fellow human being, his brother. "Lord," he prayed, "disarm me and disarm them."

On at least three other occasions, especially after the assassination of other religious to whom he was close, Father Christian recalled the possibility of his own violent death. After the Marist brother, Henri, was killed, Christian wrote:

> I was personally very close to Henri. His death seemed to be so natural, just part of a long life entirely given to the small, ordinary duties. He seemed to me to belong to the category that I call "martyrs of hope," those who are never spoken of because all their blood is poured out in patient endurance of day-to-day life. I understand "monastic martyrdom" in this same sense. It is this instinct that leads us not to change anything here at present, except for an ongoing effort at conversion. But there again, no change! (*Letter*, July 5, 1994).

After the death of the Augustinian missionaries later that year, the brothers of Atlas ratified their choice of remaining in spite of the risks. Christian wrote:

The communities of men seem to be standing by their option to remain. This is clear so far for the Jesuits, the Little Brothers of Jesus, and all the White Fathers. It is also clear for us. At Tibhirine as elsewhere, this option obviously has its risks. Each brother has told me that he wants to take these risks. For us it is a journey of faith into the future and of sharing the present with our neighbors who have always been very closely bound to us. The grace of this gift is given to us from day to day, very simply. At the end of September we had another nocturnal "visit." This time the "brothers of the mountain" wanted to use our telephone. We pretended that we were listening in.... Then we emphasized to them the contradiction that lies between our state of life and any kind of complicity with what could harm the life of another person. They gave us their assurances, but the threat of violence was there, supported by their automatic rifles (*Letter*, November 13, 1994).

Ten months later, after the assassination of the sisters of Our Lady of the Apostles, Christian wrote again:

The Pope has been so thoughtful as to send a special delegate to preside at the funeral. He is the Secretary of the Congregation for Religious. We were able to speak with him this afternoon at a meeting of bishops and major superiors. He was particularly impressive. Smiling, and with deep conviction, he confirmed us in our present situation in relation to the history of the Church, God's plan in our lives and our religious vocation, all of which include the possibility of martyrdom. He pointed out how we need to be available for that particular form of personal fidelity which the Spirit wishes to give us here and now. This does not rule out certain precautionary measures and the normal use of prudence and discretion (*Letter*, September 7, 1995).

2
Martyrs of love and faith

In the course of the twentieth century, two other communities of our order have given real martyrs of living faith to the Church and to the world: the nineteen martyrs of Our Lady of Viaceli, Spain, in 1936, and the thirty-five martyrs of Our Lady of Consolation, in China in 1947. The cause for the beatification of these martyrs has already been introduced in Rome. The seven brothers of Our Lady of Atlas have just offered us the same testimony of love and faith.

In each of these three cases we are dealing with a grace given to a community, not just to an individual person. In a cenobitic context such as that of a Cistercian monastery, the fact of a life lived and given up together is particularly meaningful. This community grace of martyrdom will also be a grace of and for the whole Church. We have already seen the love of our brothers for the Church of Algeria and for their local Church of Algiers. Their life and death is written in the register of all those religious persons, Christians and Muslims, who have lived and given their lives for God and for others.

In the Name of the Gospel

On April 27, 1996, a month after the abduction of the monks, the newspaper *Al Hayat* published extracts from Communiqué 43 of the Armed Islamic Group (GIA), dated April 18. The communiqué stated that the leader, or *Emir*, of the GIA would not recognize the *aman*, the protection, which his predecessor had granted to the monks. Moreover, this protection had not even been licit since the monks, as the communiqué reported,

> have not ceased to invite the Muslims to be evangelized. They have continued to display their Christian slogans and symbols and to commemorate their feasts with solemnity.

The *Emir* states, moreover, that monks who live among the working people can legitimately be killed.

This, he says, is the case with the monks of Atlas:

They live with the people and draw them away from the divine path, inciting them to follow the Gospel.... It is therefore licit to apply to these monks what applies to unbelievers who are prisoners of war, namely: death, slavery or exchange for Muslim prisoners.

Then comes the warning. It is this: the non-liberation of the GIA prisoners held by the French and Algerian governments will result in the death of the monks.

The choice is yours. If you liberate, we shall liberate. If you do not free your prisoners, we will cut the throats of ours. Glory to God.

It is clear from this that the brothers were condemned to death in the name of the Gospel they professed. Condemned to death for the "glory of God."

Forgiveness of Enemies

After the assassination of Brother Henri, Father Christian wrote to a group of friends:

"There is no greater love than to give one's life for those we love," said Jesus in the gospel of this May 8, 1994. If this verse sounds so applicable to the life of Brother Henri, it is not because it describes the last day of his life, but because he was essentially "given," even to the point of that perfect gift which is forgiveness. This perfect gift was already contained in the first recommendation that he had sent me for adjusting our community guidelines to the present situation. This was that in our day-to-day relations, we should openly be on the side of love, forgiveness and communion, against hate, vengeance and violence (*Letter*, May 15, 1994).

At the end of the community's annual retreat before Christmas 1994, Father Christopher summarized in his *Journal* the special points of this retreat, those that had struck him and challenged him. I could quote it all, but let us simply take this paragraph from the middle of his text:

> I see something about our particular mode of being, that is, as cenobitic monks. It resists change! It keeps going! It supports you! More specifically, take the Office: the words of the psalms resist change and become part of the situation of violence, anguish, lies and injustice. Yes, there are enemies. We cannot be forced to say too quickly that we love them, without violating our memory of the victims, the number of whom increases each day. Holy God, Strong God, come to our assistance! Make haste to help us!

For the celebration of Easter 1995 I was with the Sisters of Huambo in Angola. The civil war there was only a few months over. On Easter morning, Sister Tavita made her temporary profession. She had chosen as the Scripture reading for her profession the passage from the gospel on love of one's enemies. Trials and suffering can be crushing experiences, but they make room in our hearts for forgiveness and love of our enemies. It all has meaning, a meaning which we need to recognize and accept. Perhaps it is the discovery of this meaning which lets Christopher give Brother Luke the last word to conclude his reflections on this community retreat:

> For January 1, 1994, the beginning of the year and month of Luke's eightieth birthday, we listened in the refectory to the cassette which he was keeping to be used the day of his burial. It was Edith Piaf singing: "No, I have no regrets!"

Executed with the Lamb

I saw standing in the midst of the throne and the four living creatures and the elders, a Lamb that seemed to have been slain (Rev 5:6).

Now have salvation and power come, and the kingdom of our God and the authority of his Anointed. For the accuser of our brothers is cast out, who accuses them before our God day and night. They conquered him by the blood of the Lamb and by the word of their testimony. Love for life did not deter them from death (Rev 12:10-11).

After this I had a vision of a great multitude…. They stood before the throne and before the Lamb…. These are the ones who have survived the time of great distress. They have washed their robes and made them white in the blood of the Lamb…and the Lamb who is in the center of the throne will shepherd them and lead them to springs of life-giving water, and God will wipe away every tear from their eyes (Rev 7:9.14.17).

On May 23, 1996, we learned from the French Department of Foreign Affairs that a Moroccan radio station had broadcast a new communiqué (Number 44) from the GIA. This communiqué speaks of the execution of the seven monks of Atlas by their kidnappers. It should be read in the light of the previous communiqué and the reasons for their condemnation given there by the *emir* of the GIA. These reasons allowed for the brothers being held as slaves, their exchange for Muslim prisoners, or their murder. Since there was no exchange of prisoners being considered, the GIA has decided to apply the maximum penalty. The communiqué says:

On April 18, 1996, we published a communiqué…saying that if you set Abdelhak Layada free…, we would set the monks free, but if you refused, we would cut their throats. On April 30, 1996, we sent an emissary to the French ambassador…with an audio cassette recording to show that the monks were still alive and a written message detailing the negotiations which could be carried out if the French wished to recover their prisoners alive. At first they seemed disposed to do this and wrote us a signed and sealed letter…. Some days later, however, the French President and his Minister of Foreign Affairs declared that they would not dialogue or negotiate with the Armed Islamic Group. They cut off what they had begun and we, in fidelity to our promise, have cut the throats of the seven monks…. Glory to God…. This was done this morning, May 21.

Let the Voice of our Martyrs Resound!

The life and death of the seven monks of Atlas is a testimony not to be forgotten. May neither diplomacy, nor politics, nor a view of these events limited to this world, ever deprive us of the voice of our martyrs or silence the clamor of their cry of living faith. From the martyrdom of the spiritual combat to the martyrdom of their own blood, it is the same cry calling for forgiveness and the love of one's enemies. Life is stronger than death. Love has the last word!

As we approach both the ninth centenary of the founding of Cîteaux, in 1998, and the universal Jubilee of the Year 2000, the events surrounding our brothers of Atlas are "signs of the times" for us. They are a Word spoken by God which will not return to him without having made our hearts fertile and fruitful. Today, if you hear his voice, as persons and as communities, do not close your heart to it, but hear this pressing invitation to persevere in conversion and to advance in the all-important journey of following Jesus and his gospel. May the example of our seven brothers stir up in us the fire of love of which Saint Benedict speaks in his chapter on good zeal. May we owe nothing but love for one another, until we can even love and forgive those who have killed our brothers. It is only in this way, by forgiving and loving to this extreme, that we will be Christians, like Christian, and reach the end of our lives making our own the words of his *Testament:*

> And also you, my last-minute friend, who will not have known what you were doing:
> Yes, I want this THANK YOU and this "A-DIEU"
> to be for you, too,
> because in God's face I see yours.
> May we meet again as happy thieves in Paradise,
> if it please God, the Father of us both.
> AMEN!

> I embrace you fraternally in Mary of Saint Joseph,

Bernardo Olivera
Abbot General

CHAPTER II
Algiers and Tibhirine
Chronicle of a Celebration

June 7, 1996

Very dear Brothers and Sisters,

Yesterday I returned from Algiers. I realize that you are waiting for some news from Father Armand, our Procurator General, and myself. Although I am physically in Rome, part of me remains at Tibhirine, in the cemetery of the monastery, beside the seven graves containing the remains of our brothers.

I am at a loss as to what to tell you about everything we experienced in Algeria. The simplest way is just to share with you the notes which I took. I had thought of revising them and sending them to you in some other form, but I do not have the time and, in any case, am in no condition to do it now. So I have decided to send you this chronicle just as it was originally written. I hope that it will strengthen the bonds between all of us and the brothers of Atlas and Fes.

1
Algiers

Thursday, May 30

Armand and I left Rome at 3:25 in the afternoon on Air Algeria flight 2025. The flight was scheduled for 1:10, which means that it was two hours and fifteen minutes late. We arrived at the airport of Algiers at 3:45 local time, after an uneventful flight of an hour and twenty minutes. We were met at the airport by Father Amadeus and a Dutch Missionary of Africa, or White Father. On our arrival we were surrounded by nine plainclothes policemen who were responsible for our security. The police looked after the formalities of passport control and customs. Then, after a half hour we all went out together by a side door, since a group of French journalists from Channel Two was waiting for us at the main door. During the drive to the chancery, our car was preceded and followed by two police cars. When we arrived, we were told that a police escort would be placed at our disposal during all the time we were there. Before leaving the airport, we were informed of the death that very morning of Cardinal Duval, retired Archbishop of Algiers. He was ninety-two years old.

When we arrived at the chancery, the first person who came to greet us said, almost in a whisper, "Have you heard the news?"

"What news?" we replied.

"They have found the seven monks!"

"Alive?" we ask.

"No. Dead." Archbishop Teissier had gone to see the French ambassador, Michel Lévêque, who had told him the news only a few minutes ago.

We then passed into the archbishop's library, where there was a group of people who had come to present their condolences for the death of Cardinal Duval. Among those present was Madame Boudiaf, widow of the late president of Algeria, assassinated three years ago. The director of the newspaper *Liberté* and his wife were also there. On the faces of all these persons was etched the suffering of the Algerian people as they face the very difficult situation the country is now going through. It is difficult for me not to think of our similar experiences in Argentina during the 1970s.

Shortly after 5:00 P.M., Archbishop Teissier returned and informed us of the recent events. The authorities had told him and the ambassador that the bodies would be put in coffins which had come from Marseilles and would be taken to the Algiers Military Hospital tomorrow afternoon. When we heard this, we explained to the archbishop how important it was for us to identify the bodies of the brothers ourselves. He thought this would be impossible and said that the remains had already been identified by local people, at least it seemed so. We telephoned the ambassador to let him know our desire to identify the bodies. He thought there would be no problem. For me, as for Armand, it was a very important point.

We then broached the question of the funeral ceremony and burial. The Mass would take place in the basilica in conjunction with the funeral Mass for Cardinal Duval. The archbishop presented us with four possibilities for the burial. I told him about the desire of the brothers' families as it had been told me by Abbot Etienne of Bellefontaine during a telephone conversation that same morning. The families want the brothers to be buried all together in Algeria and, if possible, at the monastery itself. I told him that this was also the desire of our monastic family. The archbishop doubted very much whether the authorities would allow it, but we insisted on the point and finally he put us in touch with the French ambassador. The ambassador told us that the authorities would certainly make difficulties on grounds of security, but that if everything were done discreetly the authorities would give their consent.

From our arrival until after supper, the telephone never stopped ringing. We were asked to make statements for the press, radio and television. We stressed the fact that there was nothing much to say at present, but we agreed with Archbishop Teissier to organize a meeting with the reporters the next morning at nine o'clock. We feel a great sense of solidarity with the archbishop and we share his suffering. He has a very heavy cross to bear. We expressed our gratitude to him and told him that, on our part, we would be happy to help him and to lighten his burden as much as possible.

At about nine in the evening, Abbot Etienne calls and, among other things, tells me that the magazine, *Paris Match*, has mentioned the existence of a videocassette sent to the French authorities on which was shown the assassination of the brothers of Atlas. The families are in agreement in asking the authorities to destroy this film. They ask my opinion and I agree if, that is, the video really exists. Obviously, the existence of such a videotape would have political and international consequences. But let us leave that to the politicians, diplomats and magazine reporters. The job for us monks is to find the hand of God in all that happens, even if it is not easy to discern his hand among so many human hands.

Friday, May 31

The press conference took place at 9:00. Some searching questions were addressed to the archbishop, who explained the meaning of Father Christian's *Testament* and the Christian value of forgiveness. For my part, I explained the meaning of the events for our order, and the importance of the identification of the bodies. I repeated the importance of forgiveness and the fact that the request for forgiveness is a very powerful word addressed directly to the merciful heart of God, not to "human justice." Dom Armand took up the question of the recognition of the bodies which was to take place that day, then expressed the desire of both the order and the families that the monks be buried at the monastery. He added a few words on the future of the community and monastery.

At 11:00 A.M., the French ambassador, with the consul general and a young Algerian doctor from the embassy, came for us in an armored car, "us" being Archbishop Teissier, Father Amadeus of Atlas, Dom Armand and myself. We were driven to the Military Hospital of Aïn Naadja. Once we were in the car, the ambassador revealed several details about the discovery of the remains and asked us not to take photos.

When we arrived at the hospital, we were received very cordially by a group of doctors and by the director general, a colonel. They explained with great sensitivity that the brothers' death had taken place about ten days ago and that the remains had been buried, then disinterred. They thought and expected that the archbishop would simply say a prayer in the presence of the coffins, which had already been closed. For our part, we stressed the fact that we wished to identify the bodies ourselves. They replied by explaining that all the procedures required by forensic medicine in such cases had been followed, such as photographs and x-rays. The colonel added, however, that it would not be a problem to reopen the coffins so that we could carry out the identification we were asking for. He simply wanted to warn us of the emotional shock this normally produces. We told him that only some of us would carry out the identification. We asked Father Amadeus to remain in the reception room where we had entered. He somewhat grudgingly agreed and said that he would use the time to pray the office of sext.

At 12:15 we were taken to the department of forensic medicine, that is, the morgue. We decided that only the consul general who would draw up the official death certificate, the embassy doctor, Dom Armand and I would proceed to the identification. They had arranged the seven coffins in a large room very simply and discreetly. On each of the coffins was a red rose. When we saw the remains we could not help thinking of the Precursor of Jesus, St. John the Baptist. It was all over in twenty minutes.

At 1:15, we arrived at the French embassy for a meal with some other invited guests. There were several ambassadors, the apostolic nuncio and the vicar general of the diocese, Msgr. Belaïd Ould Aoudia. At the beginning of the meal Archbishop Teissier thanked the ambassador for all he had done on behalf of the monks of Tibhirine during the last two months. Dom Armand added a few words of thanks in my name and in the name of the order.

At three o'clock we returned to the chancery. The archbishop told me he was thinking of going to see the minister of the interior about the burial. I asked Dom Armand if he would accompany him in order to express, in the name of the order and the families, our desire that the monks be buried at the monastery. The archbishop agreed. They returned at 4:30 with the good news that the minister had agreed to our request. He asked only that the burial be done privately for security reasons. It would take place Tuesday morning.

At 4:40 we left again, traveling together in the two cars of the bodyguards to the Basilica of Our Lady of Africa, to pray beside the remains of Cardinal Duval. The cardinal was lying dressed all in red. I immediately thought of the seven poor coffins of our brothers, each of them with a red rose on top. On the one hand and on the other, they had all given the same testimony of peace, love and living together in harmony. At 5:30 we celebrated Mass at the basilica, then left at 6:25 to return to the chancery. I found a reporter waiting for me, one who specializes in matters concerning Islam. He told me with great emotion of his deep personal pain and that of the Algerian people in the face of what had happened to our brothers. Meanwhile, Dom Armand had gone to the studio of Channel One for a live broadcast to

France on the 8:00 P.M. Telenews. He announced, among other things, that the burial would take place at the monastery on the following Tuesday.

Saturday, June 1

We stayed at the chancery all day. Before lunch the archbishop told us the latest news: the minister of the interior had decided that next Tuesday we would only be a small group of about ten people going to Tibhirine with the coffins, and we would go by helicopter. This was for reasons of security and to avoid the presence of crowds and reporters.

After lunch I was able to meet with Father Amadeus for a very long time, almost three hours. We went through the contents of a small suitcase with all the personal documents of the brothers. I chose recent photographs of each of them in order to make copies and send them to their next of kin. I advised Amadeus to preserve all this documentation very carefully, because it would certainly be useful and necessary one day. We also discussed other practical questions concerning plans for the future and for the monastery.

From 6:00 P.M. on, those who had been invited began to arrive for the funeral the next day: Cardinal Arinze as papal delegate, the four bishops of Algeria and seven members of Father Christopher's family. There was Élisabeth and François, Vincent and Thérèse, Claire, Xavier and Madame Finot, Brother Christopher's godmother. I felt that the Lebreton family understood the deep significance of the events better than many other people. It is an example of that mysterious, prophetic *"sensus fidelium"* among God's people! They gave me a copy of three recent poems by Christopher. I extract from each of these poems certain phrases that seem to me to be especially enlightening, such as these:

> I belong to Him and, walking his way, I go toward my full Easter truth.

> Seeing the road that the turn of events is taking,
> I tell you truly, it's all right.

> The flame has bent over
> the light has slanted
> I can die
> and here I am.

Sunday, June 2

During the morning, I prepared the "testimony" I had been asked for, to read during the Mass this evening. I gave it to Father P.L.* to read and he gave his full agreement to it. Then we read it together with Father Amadeus. Here it is:

What can a monk say about his brother monks? I know, as they did, that our charism in the Church is to be silent, work, intercede and praise God. But we know, too, that there are times to speak, as there are times to keep silence.

The hidden voice of the monks remained silently in the cloisters of Our Lady of Atlas for more than fifty years. This voice was changed during the last two months into a cry of love which has echoed in the hearts of millions of believers and persons of good will. Our seven brothers of Tibhirine—Christian, Luke, Christopher, Michael, Bruno, Celestine and Paul—are transformed today into spokesmen for all those stifled voices and unknown persons who have given their life for a more humane world. Our seven monks lend their voice to me, too, today.

The monks' testimony, like that of every believing Christian, can only be understood as a prolongation of the testimony of Christ himself. Our life following Christ should manifest with total clarity the divine liberality of the good news of the gospel which we desire to live. This good news is that a life given and offered is never lost. It is always found again in Him who is the Life.

---

*Initials have been changed for the protection of those involved in the events related in this book.

We must enter into the world of the other, whether that person be Christian or Muslim. In fact if the "other" does not exist as such, there is no space for true love. We need to be disturbed and enriched by the existence of the other. Let us remain open and sensitive to every voice that challenges us. Let us choose love, forgiveness and communion against every form of hatred, vengeance and violence. Let us believe without flinching in the deep desire for peace which resides in the depth of every human heart.

Our brother monks are a ripe fruit of this Church which is living the paschal mystery in Algeria. Our brother monks are also a ripe fruit of this people of Algeria who received them and esteemed their life during these many years of presence and communion. For this reason, I want to express a word of thanks on our part to all of you. Church of Algeria, all you Algerians, adorers of the one God: a heartfelt *thank you* for the respect and love you have shown for our brother monks.

> Listen, if you can possibly listen:
> To come to Him is to leave oneself.
> Silence: up there is the world of vision.
> For them, our monks of Tibhirine, the word is only
> Seeing.
> Amen.

When the moment came to name each brother, Amadeus and I had to stop reading. Tears full of love gave us eyes of glory to see the invisible. We bowed our heads in silent prayer.

Around 11:30 I had a good meeting with L.M., a close friend of Christian. I asked him to send me in writing his experience of the night of March 27. He promised to do so that very day. I also asked him for an explanation of the theme they had worked on together at Easter 1995, in the *Ribat* meeting. This is the Islam-Christian dialogue group which met periodically for prayer in the monastic context of Tibhirine. He explained that the theme was: "O God, You are our Hope." Father Christopher had added in his commentary: "on the Face of all the Living." He sent me a copy of Christopher's complete text and so I was able to read it. Christopher had written:

> We have this theme: You on the Face of all the Living. If I pray it and seek to understand it, so as to bring my heart and mind into agreement with what I am saying and with what the Spirit wants to say in me, I first discover that I am the one whose face is seen by You [*en-visagé de Toi*] from among all the living. I am the chosen one who is looked upon by You and loved, if I am willing…. But then what about the others? For all of them to become a face, You will have to see the face of each one.

All this is linked with the last lines of Christian's *Testament*:

> And also you, my last-minute friend, who will not have known what you were doing: Yes, I want this THANK YOU and this "A-DIEU" to be for you, too, because in God's face I see yours [*en-visagé de toi*].

I explained to L.M. how I understood Christian's *Testament*. He listened with tears in his eyes, then he said, "Yes, that's right."

• The *Testament* begins, "When we have to face an A-DIEU" (*Quand un A-DIEU s'envisage*), that is, in the context of a possible departure which only God can know.

• Christian continues, "I should like, when the time comes, …to forgive with all my heart the one who will strike me down."

• Then he comes to the moment of death: "Finally my most avid curiosity will be satisfied…immerse my gaze in that of the Father and contemplate with him His children of Islam as He sees them, ...filled with the Gift of the Spirit, whose secret joy will always be to establish communion and restore the likeness, delighting in the differences...."

- This contemplation, however, is anticipated at the very moment of death. That is why Christian can find his "last-minute friend," his assassin, reflected in the face of God: "in God's face I see yours" [*en-visagé de toi*].

- This is a difficult, yet important, phrase to understand. Christian is playing with words, like the poet that he was. Grammatically, the only really clear elements are that he is directly addressing his assassin and that he divides the word, *envisager*, in order to emphasize *visage*, face.

- However, one of the primary rules of interpretation is that the meaning of a difficult text should be judged according to its context. Here, as we have just seen, the context is one of contemplating with the Father "his children of Islam as he sees them." This shows that Christian was a true mystic, someone who saw persons and the world as they are in God, even more than a prophet, who sees God in persons and the world. Thus his thought is interpreted better as "in God's face I see yours" rather than "in your face I see God's."

- The *Testament* ends when forgiveness has brought about transformation and restored God's likeness. God the Father and one's human neighbor are found in one and the same act. This is the deep mystery of love and the prolongation of the Love of Christ who died saying, "Father, forgive them for they do not know what they are doing."

At 12:30 we leave for *Les Glycines*, the diocesan cultural center, to have lunch with Archbishop Teissier, the papal nuncio and Cardinal Arinze. I take advantage of this visit to inspect, with the director of the center, the room where they are storing many items belonging to the monastery: the prior's archives, the personal papers of the brothers, holy pictures, the crozier, a chalice and paten, and so forth. I take some things that were in Father Christopher's three boxes to give to his sisters and brothers: an envelope with family photos, a notebook with souvenirs of his ordination, a New Testament, two *Jerusalem Bibles*: one a pocket edition, the other normal size. At 2:00 P.M. we are back at the chancery.

At 2:50 they came again in the armored car of the French embassy to take us to the military hospital, where we were to pick up the seven coffins and take them to the Basilica of Our Lady of Africa. We go there together: Father Amadeus, Dom Armand, Father G. N. and myself. We arrive in twenty minutes. The colonel is waiting for us and receives us most cordially. We go together to the department of forensic medicine. A guard of thirty military cadets with shining helmets put the coffins into four yellow ambulances. Everything was done with great respect and dignity. At 3:35 we leave for the basilica accompanied by an impressive security guard of three motorcycles, three patrol cars, two military vans and a fire truck. They had taken care to stop the traffic along the whole way. During the twenty-five minute drive, Father Amadeus devoutly recites his rosary.

We arrived at the basilica at 4:00. Many reporters, along with radio and television crews, were waiting for us. There was a surge of deep emotion when our seven brothers were carried into the basilica. A few minutes later, Cardinal Lustiger and three French bishops arrived, one of whom was Archbishop Duval, president of the Episcopal Conference of France and nephew of Cardinal Duval. In the sacristy I found Father Jean-Pierre of Atlas and Father R.F., who had just arrived from Fes and Tibhirine respectively. Since the civil authorities, that is, the five ministers representing the Algerian government, had arrived a little early, we decided to begin the funeral Mass for Cardinal Duval and our seven brothers at once. It was 4:40 P.M. The eight coffins filled the sanctuary. On each one had been placed a big wreath of flowers and a large photograph. Cardinal Duval and the monks were united once more. It had not been in vain that the cardinal had prevented the Trappist Order from closing the monastery at the beginning of the 1960s! Cardinal Arinze, the Pope's delegate, presided at the celebration, with Archbishops Teissier and Duval on either side, immediately followed by myself, Dom Armand, Father Amadeus and Father Jean-Pierre. It was deeply moving to see on the altar the chalice and paten of the monastery, inlaid as they were, with coral from Kabyle. The celebration proceeded according to plan, except that the message of President Chirac on the occasion of the death of the brothers was replaced by a telegram of condolence from the Pope on the death of Cardinal Duval.

By 6:30, the long Mass was over. Many people approached us to greet us with tears in their eyes. One of the security guards at the military hospital, a Muslim, shook my hand effusively saying, "The monks are our brothers, too." Many asked our forgiveness for what had happened. All I could say was, "Thank you." I met the Argentine ambassador: Gerónimo Cortes-Funes, a high school friend of my older brother. What a small world! Armand and I blessed the remains of our brothers one last time and, at about 7:00 P.M., left the basilica to return to the chancery.

At about 7:30, Armand goes to the French embassy for a meal with the ecclesiastical authorities. I ask him to give my apologies to the ambassador. I prefer to stay at the house and have supper with Father Amadeus, Father Jean-Pierre and the family of Father Christopher. After the meal, I gave the Lebreton family what had belonged to Christopher, from among the items I had brought from *Les Glycines* that morning. It has been a long day, filled with restrained emotion.

Monday, June 3

At 7:30 we celebrate the Eucharist, with Cardinal Lustiger presiding. We were about thirty persons in all, the little flock remaining from the once large diocese of Algiers. Before the last blessing, the cardinal thanks all present for "the faith of this small local church which gives life and support to the decadent faith of old Europe."

After Mass I ask Father Amadeus if it would be possible to go to *Les Glycines* and get the boxes containing Christopher's personal effects. I would like his family to inspect the contents and take the more personal souvenirs to Madame Lebreton, Christopher's mother. After lunch, I met L.M. again and he gave me the account I had asked for two days ago. It consists of six pages describing the whole experience at the monastery in the early morning of March 27 and throughout that day. I remind Fathers Amadeus and Jean-Pierre that I am waiting for their own account of those events.

From 3:00 to 4:30 this afternoon, I had a good meeting with Fathers Amadeus and Jean-Pierre. There were various practical points to be dealt with and some decisions to be made. We went over the program for the burial at the monastery. Is it possible to maintain a presence at Tibhirine for two or three years in view of coming back if the situation in the country returns to normal? I offer them whatever financial help is needed to look for a house in Medea for the gate keeper and his family, if he wishes to move. I remind Jean-Pierre that, as the appointed superior of the community, he would have to come to Rome for the next General Chapter. Finally, we speak about Father Michael, a Dominican priest who has asked for a transfer to our order and wishes to enter at Fes.

At about 5:00 in the afternoon I meet with Claire and Father Amadeus, to go through Christopher's personal papers. Soon Élisabeth and Xavier arrived. It was not easy to distinguish between notes from his studies, conference notes, personal journals and poems. There were also many letters he had received, which we decided to burn out of respect for the persons who had sent them. We put all the photos together to send to Madame Lebreton. I took for myself a large notebook containing a personal journal. On the first page is written: "Prayer Notebook begun this Sunday, August 8, 1993 at Tibhirine." The last entry in this journal is for March 19, 1996, a week before the kidnapping. I read:

> Saint Joseph. Bruno and Father J.C. arrived yesterday. Today is the anniversary of my consecration to Mary. Yes, I continue to choose you, Mary, with Joseph, in the communion of all the saints, and I receive you from the hands of Jesus with the poor and the sinners. Like the beloved disciple, I take you into my home. Near you, I am what I should be: offered. In the garden this morning, a good discussion with M.S. on marriage. I was happy to preside at the Eucharist. It was as if I heard the voice of Joseph inviting me to sing Psalm 100 with him and the child: "My song is of mercy and justice…. I will walk in the way of perfection. O when, Lord, will you come? I will walk with blameless heart."

Among his many poems, there is one that is very significant in the light of all that has happened. Unfortunately, it has no date, but it would not be difficult to establish its approximate time of composition. Here it is:

testament

> *my body is for the earth*
> *so please*
> *no preservatives*
> *just earth and me*

my heart was made for life
so please
no affectation
    just life and me

my hands were made for work
they fold
    quite simply

as for my face
uncover it
    for an easier kiss

and for my gaze
let it SEE

P.S.
    thank you.

After supper we meet with Élisabeth, Claire and Xavier to explain to them the circumstances surrounding the discovery and identification of the brothers' remains. After giving a brief introduction, I ask Armand to speak. It was very painful for both us and them, but the pain brought us all together on a deep level. We ended by praying together in silence in the chapel on the second floor.

2

Burial

Tuesday, June 4

The day began early. Before 7:00 A.M. we phoned Christopher's mother, thinking that we would console her, but it was she who consoled us. I told her she now had 4,500 new sons and daughters, all the Trappists. She replied, "I feel I am truly the mother of them all." I am sure that the mothers of each of the seven brothers, whether living or dead, on earth or in heaven, are all saying the same thing.

At 7:30, the ambassador came to get us in his armored car and we were all driven to the airport: the archbishop; Élisabeth, Claire and Xavier from the Lebreton family; Amadeus and Jean-Pierre of Atlas; Armand and I from the order as a whole. We were going to the monastery, but did not know exactly how. There was a great turnout of security guards at the airport. At nine o'clock all of us, with six members of the guard, boarded a military plane which, at the end of a thirty-minute flight, landed us at the air base of Ain Oussera, seventy-five miles south of Medea. A helicopter was to have flown us to Medea, but the bad weather prevented it. At a little before 10:00, we left for the monastery with an escort of more than twelve pickup trucks full of armed soldiers. A helicopter flew directly above our convoy during the entire first part of the journey.

We arrived at Atlas at noon. The ambulances with the mortal remains of our brothers were already there. The weather was wet and overcast. All nature seemed to be weeping for sorrow. There was a great display of police and military at Medea and even more at the monastery. Our little group of nine went to the church where T.L. and Father R.F. were waiting for us. The coffins were carried by about thirty military cadets, all with great respect and dignity. Behind closed doors and in total privacy, I presided over a simple liturgy: a few words of welcome, a song ("*Souviens-toi de Jésus-Christ*"), a prayer in the form of a litany ("You who by the water of baptism sanctified our brothers Christian, Luke, Christopher, Michael, Celestine, Bruno and Paul, give them in its fullness the life of God's children"), a reading from the gospel ("Today you will be with me in Paradise"), sprinkling with holy water, incensing and a concluding prayer. Xavier was the thurifer. Armand and Élisabeth took some photos. Then we opened the doors once again and the cadets entered to carry the mortal remains to the community cemetery.

The seven graves had been prepared. The coffins of the brothers were placed in front of their respective graves: first Christian, then the others in order of monastic seniority. Father Jean-Pierre addressed a few words of thanks full of hope to all those present—neighbors and authorities. Then the archbishop and Father R.Q. spoke in Arabic. I said a final prayer and then they began to lower the coffins into the graves. It was already 1:15. The archbishop cast the first shovelful of earth into the grave of Michael and I into that of Christopher. A group of neighbors continued the task. At that very moment the sun broke through the clouds. The coffins disappeared under the earth, and we disappeared beneath the embraces, kisses and condolences of countless neighbors of the monastery, who at the same time thanked us for having buried the monks here. At 1:45 it was all over. We stopped briefly in a room of the monastery where the prefect of Medea had prepared tables with coffee, tea and candied fruit. Taking advantage of the general confusion, I made a rapid visit through the monastery. I took a Christ in olive wood which was hanging on the wall of the library, with the idea of sending it to Madame Lebreton. A single phrase was resounding in my heart: "We will not leave our dead alone, we shall come back!" We left at 2:00 P.M.—without leaving.

The return journey was slightly different. We went by car as far as the military base of Berouaghia, from there by helicopter to the air base of Ain Oussera, and finally in the military plane back to Algiers. At 4:45 we were back at the chancery. At 5:00, we celebrated a Eucharist with the prayers and readings of Easter Day. The texts of Easter expressed our feelings well. Father Jean-Pierre presided.

After the Mass I met again with Géronimo Cortes-Funes, the Argentine ambassador, who had come to present his condolences. We spent a long time together discussing different religious, political and social questions. After supper, Jean-Pierre and Armand met with the families in order to share with them what they had experienced during the day. For my part, I called Dom Etienne of Bellefontaine who told me that the mother and sister of Christian were there; I asked him to convey my most affectionate remembrance to them.

Wednesday, June 5

Xavier left at 6:30 in the morning and after Mass, at 7:30, Élisabeth and Claire departed. It is incredible how the victorious death of Christopher and the other brothers of Tibhirine has united us to their families.

It was already nine o'clock when I met with Jean-Pierre to talk about the future of Fes. It is clear that the community there is the community of Atlas, presently living at Fes. The average age of the community is very high and their health not good, but their spirits are excellent. As for the future, what seems clear is, first, they should try to return to Tibhirine as soon as possible. Secondly, they need volunteers to come from other communities of the order. And thirdly, it may be necessary to leave the present residence of Fes because of its restricted living space. In order to help the community materially and spiritually, it might be good to name a small *ad hoc* commission composed of Father Jean-Pierre, an abbot and a permanent councillor.

At about 2:30 that afternoon, Father J.C., the parish priest of Our Lady of the Nativity since 1971, came to greet me. He is a close friend of the community and was the "father" of Christopher's monastic vocation. He told me what had happened during his last visit to the monastery, on March 19. To his great surprise, the brothers had prepared a triple celebration: for his seventy-ninth birthday on March 15, for the feast of his patron saint, Joseph, and for his golden jubilee of priesthood. As a present they gave him the *Book of Revelations* of Julian of Norwich. The brothers had stamped the first page with the seal of the monastery and around the seal had written, in red letters, the words: "Tout finira bien. Alleluia." These words, "All shall be well," express the theme that is constantly repeated by the mystic. During the two months of the brothers' captivity, Father J.C. wondered about the meaning of these words. Concretely, how can everything be well? The obvious answer was an alternative: either through giving glory to God by accepting death and offering it to him, or by living and glorifying God in daily monastic life. Now there is only one answer. And the good priest added, "Never in all my life have I experienced such peace and felt so close to God as I do now. Tibhirine is a grace for us all, both the Christians in Algeria and the Algerian people as a whole. Time will show this to be true more and more. We needed martyrs, now we have them." Later he sent me the text of Christopher's homily for the feast of Saint Joseph, which was most probably his last one.

With Armand's help I prepare three letters. The first is for the brothers of Fes, to encourage them and to clarify their present situation as an autonomous community of the order. The second letter is for the minister of the interior, to thank him for all his help during the course of the past week, with visas, transportation, security and the like. The third one is for the French ambassador, to thank him for his untiring devotion during the two preceding months. It seems to me to be very important to find and meet the human person existing under the official titles and institutional functions.

After supper, Archbishop Teissier, Jean-Pierre, Armand and I met again. The principal questions were the upkeep of the buildings, the safety of the gatekeeper, the situation of the community of Fes (I gave him a copy of the letter I had written to the brothers there), the community archives and personal writings of the monks which are at *Les Glycines* (I suggest that everything be kept there as long as possible and necessary, since these things belong to this local Church, too). We prayed compline with the archbishop in his chapel and thus ended our last day in Algiers. We leave tomorrow morning, God willing.

Thursday, June 6

At 6:30 we begin to say good-bye to everyone at the chancery. It is amazing how such strong bonds could be established in such a short time. The blood of our martyred brothers has deeply united us with the Church that suffers and rejoices in Algeria. The seven martyrs are our brothers, but also their brothers. As martyrs, they belong to Algeria as well as to us. Please God, they will be the last martyrs to shed their blood for a long time.

Father P.L. drives us to the airport. We are escorted by the bodyguard that had been assigned to us the day we arrived. At 10:08, Flight 2024 of Air Algeria, takes off for Rome. During the flight I close my eyes. All sorts of faces and images pass through my imagination. We have experienced so much! I ask our seven martyrs, "What message do you have for the order?" I read the reply in their lives:

- They followed Jesus to the end, in the absolutely radical living of the Gospel.

- They plunged into his mystery, to the point of being totally transformed by him.

- They lived together, died together and went together into eternal Life.

- They shared in their intimate communion with the universal Church and their own local Church.

- They were in deep solidarity with the men and women of today.

- They discerned the signs of the times and the nature of contemporary challenges.

- They enriched our patrimony from a specific cultural context.

• They sealed with their own blood their openness and commitment to interreligious dialogue.

At 12:30 local time, we landed at Fiumicino Airport, Rome. Father André was waiting for us.

Bernardo Olivera
Abbot General

CHAPTER III
Their Story and Ours

Into the Mystery

October 12, 1996

Very dear Brothers and Sisters,

Three days after the martyrdom of our seven brothers I received a letter from Dom Ignace Gillet, a former Abbot General. In this letter, which concerned the recent events, Dom Ignace wrote, "There seems to be a current of new life in our monasteries.... I myself clearly sense that I am not the same as before." These words were written by a venerable monk of ninety-five who knows the order as few of us do, so they carry a special weight of meaning.

There is no denying that a powerful current of witnessing to the gospel has passed through the order during recent months: a living stream that gives life, encourages, wakes us up, stimulates us and carries us back to our first love. I too have felt shaken up and brought to new life. I can say the same thing as Dom Ignace: I sense that I am not the same as before. I am 50 years older and 103 years younger!

In this letter I wish to return to the grace which has come to us through our brothers, our seven witnesses in him who is *the* Witness, our mediators in the one Mediator. Going back over the events will help us recognize the goodness and power of the one Lord of history. It will help convert our hearts to be like his.

Let us go back, then, over the years and let the Lord speak to us through the facts. We will read the story in the light of faith, so that it clearly becomes part of our own salvation history. Above all, we will let our brothers explain what happened, both those who are still with us on our pilgrim journey and those who wait for us in God's kingdom.

1
The Background

Algeria did not Begin Yesterday

On July 5, 1830, the French fleet landed on the coast of Algeria and conquered the territory by force of arms. Almost immediately it was annexed to France. A great number of French colonists emigrated to Algerian territory. Thirteen years later, in 1843, a group of twelve monks from Aiguebelle settled at Staouéli, west of Algiers, and thus the Cistercian adventure began anew in Africa. The monastery of Our Lady of Atlas was founded in 1934 from what was then called Yugoslavia, by the Abbey of Our Lady of Liberation. After several unsuccessful attempts in different places, it was finally established in Tibhirine as a daughter house of Aiguebelle.

Soon afterwards, in 1938, Ferhat Abbas founded the "Algerian Popular Union." It was a movement aimed at independence based on Algeria's Arabic heritage. Five years later, in 1943, he asked the French governor for recognition of an independent and sovereign Algerian state. France's refusal provided the occasion for open opposition to French domination. In 1945, after the Second World War, France tried to suppress any attempt towward Algerian independence. This led to open war against France, which began in 1954. The Algerians were led by Ben Bellá, Ait Ahmed and Mohammed Kedir. In July 1959, two members of the Atlas community, Father Matthew and Brother Luke, were kidnapped, then set free eight days later.

The signing of Algeria's independence took place on March 18, 1962. Its official proclamation came less than four months later, on July 3. On September 8, Ben Bellá of the National Liberation Front (FLN), was elected as the country's president.

The 1965 chronicle of the Abbey of Atlas tells how the previous year it had almost been decided to close the monastery. The General Chapter of January 1964 issued the verdict that

> The Most Reverend Father General and the Assembly would be happy if a monastery of the Order would offer to take upon itself the refounding of Atlas. If this does not happen, the closing of the house will take place according to the principle already decided by the Definitory.

Archbishop Duval of Algiers persistently opposed this decision. His trust was limitless. "The desert will bloom again," he wrote to the Abbot of Timadeuc, who had decided to send some monks to the African abbey. On October 29, 1964, while visiting Atlas, the archbishop was able to update his statement: "The desert has already bloomed."

On June 19, 1965, President Ben Bellá was deposed by a *coup d'état*. A revolutionary council took over, headed by Colonel Bumedien, who was later elected president. On June 27, 1976, the National Charter was promulgated. It states that Algeria is a socialist country following the Islamic religion and speaking Arabic. Bumedien died two years later, on December 27, 1978. A month afterwards, on January 31, 1979, the congress of the FLN elected Benjedid Chadli as president. He was reelected in 1984 by a general election.

During the last ten years there was an increase in fundamentalist groups and in those unsatisfied with the National Charter of 1976. In the context of many political parties, one of these groups, the Islamic Salvation Front (FIS), was successful in the administrative elections of June 1990. Seeing this success, the FIS demanded general political elections which would take place on June 27, 1991. Civil disorder delayed the elections until December 26. In the first round the FIS obtained 24% of the votes. The army intervened to suspend the second round, which would have taken place on June 16, 1992. President Chadli was deposed and power was assumed by the High Commission of State (HCE) presided over by Mohamed Boudiaf. The FIS was declared illegal and all political activity was suspended. Now that they were obliged to go underground, the most radical wing of the FIS, the Armed Islamic Group (GIA), began an uninterrupted chain of terrorist acts. On June 29, 1992, President Boudiaf was assassinated.

2
An Unexpected Letter

Where Have You Led Me?

It was January 17, 1994. Among the many letters that came that morning was a big envelope on which were some Algerian stamps and the small handwriting of Father Christian. I opened the envelope and read:

Dear Father and brother Bernardo,

Herewith a whole dossier to give a full account of the events. It was difficult to get in touch with the generalate to tell you these things. Everything happened very quickly, including our own community discussion of "preferences." After the visit of Christmas night, there was a very understandable reaction of immediate "flight." I was perhaps best placed to know that if there was a threat; it fell first of all on me, because I was, and am, the "password": a really lucky destiny! In the immediate future I do not think that the community as a whole runs the risk of suffering the atrocious death of our friends of Tamesguida. But how can we avoid keeping their image in our minds?

Now there is a real calm., a peace that comes from the Child and his Mother. There is also the hope which the neighbors attach to our presence as a spiritual buffer between the two armed forces.

Along with the handwritten letter, there were also several other documents with different titles:

- Chronology of events

- Situation on January 5, 1994 (at 6:00 A.M.)

- Community Votes—December 31, 1993 (confidential)

- Brother Christian de Chergé, Prior of the Monastery of Tibhirine, to the Honorable Prefect of Medea, December 30, 1993.

- Report by Brother Christopher

I understood immediately that something important had happened, something we very much hoped would not. I picked up the telephone and spoke personally with Christian. His voice was peaceful. He explained what happened. I sensed that something new had started at Our Lady of Atlas. After speaking with him I returned to reading the documents:

Chronology of events

- *October 1993*: Three officers of the French consulate are taken as hostages. Released, they are bearers of a distinct threat from the GIA (Armed Islamic Group) aimed at all foreigners living in Algeria: all foreigners "have one month to leave the country." Many ambassadors take the warning very seriously (German, Belgian, British…). France does not want to risk leaving Algeria, but advises prudence.

- *November 17, 1993*: Brother Christian is summoned to the Cabinet of the *Wali* [prefect]. They suggest a police guard. He absolutely refuses any armed presence. He merely agrees no longer to open the gates at night.

- *December 1, 1993*: The month of grace allowed to foreigners expires. Very soon a Spaniard, a Frenchman, a Russian woman (of mixed blood) and a Briton…are assassinated.

- *December 14, 1993*: At nightfall, twelve (out of nineteen) ex-Yugoslavians, mainly Croatians, from an hydraulic plant installed in Tamesguida (nine miles as the crow flies from the monastery, right next door) have their throats slit by a commando force estimated at fifty persons. Two Croats miraculously escape the slaughter. The victims were picked out for being Christians and Croatians no doubt with reference to the present conflict with Bosnia. We used to receive them as visitors each year on Christmas and Easter night. It is a real shock for the community.

- *December 19, 1993*: Brother Christian is summoned once more to the *Wilaya* [prefecture]. There is an hour-long interview in the office of the *Wali*, who is anxious to take security measures to protect the community after the massacre of Tamesguida. He suggests that we "take a holiday in France" or retire to a "protected hotel" in

Medea for the night at the expense of the *Wilaya*, or have more arms, etc. Such measures are clearly not appropriate, especially to the religious state. There is a feeling in community that the danger is not going to get any less, that any temporary departure in these conditions would run the risk of being without possibility of return and that our neighbors would not understand. We agree to improve the telephone line and a new number is installed the same day. We will also be more sensitive to indications coming from round about. We have no illusions and we decide to lock ourselves in at night more securely and earlier. We are also aware of being in somewhat exceptional conditions of monastic *conversatio* and that we should avoid what the *Wali* called "collective suicide." We reaffirm our reasons for remaining. We see that we are at the juncture between two groups who are in confrontation here and, to some extent, everywhere in the West and Near East.

- *December 24, 1993*: At about 7:15 in the evening, "they" are here: three inside our walls and three others outside, all armed but without directly threatening anything or anyone. They burst into the guest house where our parish priest, R.Q., and three African students are with the guest master, Brother Paul. They ask to see "the pope of the place." One of them comes into the cloister and tries to assemble the brothers, two of whom flee without being seen and will remain hidden until vigils, fearing the worst. Brother Christian goes to the guest house. He has a long interview with the one in charge, pointing out that this is the first time that weapons are coming into our "house of peace," where they have no place. The chief wishes to reassure us of his good intentions, both now and for the future, but he lays down three conditions: 1...2...3. Brother Christian argues with him. The chief replies, "You have no choice." However, they have not realized that it was Christmas. They are confused. Their aim is clearly to compromise us. It was impossible to contact the authorities. Obviously, this is a rather special Christmas!

- *December 26, 1993*: We hold a community meeting. A majority of the brothers are in favor of an immediate departure. They doubt that there is any time left to make provision for the future. We are unanimous in thinking that it is not moral to satisfy their demand to help their revolutionary movement. It would be a commitment that would be very difficult for the Church to assume. However, one of the Christmas visitors clearly pointed out that the GIA made a distinction between "Christians" and "foreigners."

- *December 27, 1993*: We receive a visit from our archbishop, Father Teissier. As he places our community in its context, he emphasizes the effect which our sudden departure would have on all the Christians who face the same trial. He suggests something "by stages," which would provide for a transition period in relation to the surrounding area and would safeguard the future. But he stops short of insisting on such a decision.

- *December 28, 1993*: The community comes around to the bishop's point of view. Three brothers will depart provisionally for reasons of anxiety or for studies. The others will prepare for a departure in the future. In the evening, the bishop goes to inform the *Wali* of something.

- *December 29, 1993*: Brother Christian is summoned to the *Wilaya*. He is given a strong letter from the *Wali* recalling the need for security measures and disclaiming his responsibility for any future tragedy. He asks for an answer.

- *December 30, 1993*: The community answers the *Wali*.

• *December 31, 1993*: We take a series of community votes to clarify our decisions and the paths open for the future. There is a very strong consensus in favor of refusing "collaboration" and proceeding by stages, keeping open the possibility of remaining if there is no obstacle, especially because of our ignorance concerning what the promised "envoy" of the mountaineers might ask. We also want to remain together, and to provide for a return to Algeria. Fes is a halfway house.

The sheet entitled, *Situation on January 5, 1994*, attracts my attention. I read: 1, 2, 3, 4, 5, 6 and come to paragraphs 7 and 8:

7. In community we have lived through an experience of deep communion, moment after moment, receiving the words of our common prayer and the elements of the regular life as a true gift from God dictating to us what we should say and do, here and now. Brother Luke, doctor and senior, has a fundamental role!

8. For several weeks, therefore, just six of us are going to remain here. The season is more favorable to this reduced number. The guest house is temporarily closed. We can count on the support of the associates who are more directly linked to the management of the property under the supervision of Brother Christopher. On the material level, we are going to have to tighten our belts in order to make ends meet, just like our neighbors.

My interest and understanding of the situation grow as I read. I feel as if I were at Tibhirine myself. Now it is Christopher speaking to me as I read his *Report*:

This Christmas has not been like any other.
It is still charged with meaning.

Like Mary, we ponder these things that have happened to us. We continue the inner conversation she began in her heart. The meaning pierces us like a sword. The Word takes on this community of body and blood to speak here, today, Himself.

We have just finished our community retreat with Father Sanson, S.J. He had points for examination of conscience and points for prayer. Each one of us has no doubt made a few good resolutions. I had none other than yours: the resolution of committed love. Each day I receive it, I take it, I eat it, I drink it. This is my body which is given up for you. This is the cup of my blood shed for you and for all.

This is my resolution: to live through Him, with Him, in Him.

We are in a situation of *epiclesis*.

I am learning a few things, especially that the school of the Lord's service does not go on Christmas vacation. The Child is our Teacher. I am learning what it means to be Church: the great happiness of being physically held in this body which gives voice to the Presence in the here and now.

THE LOVE WHO COMES

Present with us that night were R., our parish priest and three African students. There were those men and women from Croatia and Bosnia who had come for the feast of Christmas 1991.

I am learning what it means to be Church. I see her adorned as a Bride for her Husband, the Suffering Servant.

Fernand was also present, a friend from Savoy.

There we were, each one of us, living through the events which have brought us so close to each other, without erasing any of the differences. In the morning we admitted that it would be idiotic to try to reach a consensus.

Each of us has experienced such deep realities. Each of us gives them a personal interpretation. Each one tries to integrate them. And there is also a "we" who journey together, growing in wisdom and grace (!?!). We have been uprooted and led to a place where we could never have gone despite all our religious training.

The Mystery of Faith is deep, that of more loving fidelity. Yes, I am moved at being a member of this body, which has neither majesty nor beauty.

Henri Teissier, our diocesan shepherd, came to visit us. His first act was to preside over our Sacrifice of Praise. Afterwards, we listened to him and let ourselves take in the depth of the anxiety of a shepherd whose sheep are threatened. He left again, leaving us free in a situation to which there was no obvious solution. We have also had to learn obedience together, without any personal agenda, respecting the conscience of each person.

I am also learning something else. It is a point on which much has been written, and I have had my own ideas on the subject: it is the question of monks. I'm learning that there is first of all the Church, and that we belong to this body of Christ. I know that we are not better people, nor heroes, nor indeed anything extraordinary. I feel this very strongly here at Tibhirine. And yet, there is something unique in our way of being Church: how we react to events, how we wait for them and live them out in practice. It has to do with a certain awareness that we are responsible not for doing something, but for being something here, in response to Truth and to Love. Are we facing eternity? There is a sense of that. "Our Lady of Atlas, a sign on the mountain," *signum in montibus*, as our coat of arms declares.

I see something about our particular mode of being, that is, as cenobitic monks. It resists change! It keeps going! It supports you! More specifically, take the Office: the words of the psalms resist change and become part of the situation of violence, anguish, lies and injustice. Yes, there are enemies. We cannot be forced to say too quickly that we love them, without violating our memory of the victims, the number of whom increases each day. Holy God, Strong God, come to our assistance! Make haste to help us!

We also receive words of encouragement and consolation, words that give us hope. It is here that reading the Scriptures is vital. There is meaning. It must be received and acknowledged. Then, being acknowledged, it is accomplished. You who come! This is full of meaning for us now. It is being accomplished. Love is in the shape of a Cross.

There is a person whose role is clearly highlighted in the Rule of Saint Benedict. It is the abbot. Yes, we believe that he holds the place of You who give Your life. This role is held by one of us. He has received the special, basically secular, title of "Monsieur Christian," that is, the password, the word of Passover. This gentleman is the link with Mary: "I alone will pass." In him, filial and fraternal solitude are close to the Mother. It is a difficult mission. It weighs upon him and upon each one of us. We are a little overwhelmed, a little worn down. We go to bed earlier! The work, of course, is one of faith!

Monks. We are in the process of becoming a little more truly monks according to the gospel of our Lord Jesus Christ, and this is spiritual inculturation. The symbiosis with our neighbors, with the country, has great benefits for us. It gives us the vision to see. For example, there is the look of A. when night comes and he returns home, leaving us until tomorrow, *inch'Allah!* There is W.R. trimming an apple tree with T.L. yesterday, feast of the Epiphany, or the meeting with the associates to mark the

New Year. M.H. taking up his new responsibility as deputy chief of agriculture.

Excuse me for going on like this, but there is still something else. It is about eating and drinking together. Ah, the french fries of toubib...delivered only by special order...like honey from the rock! Brother Luke? Yes, he is very exposed. On January 1, 1994, the beginning of the year and month of Luke's eightieth birthday, we listened in the refectory to the cassette he was keeping to be used the day of his burial. It was Edith Piaf singing: "No, I have no regrets!"

Rereading Christopher's *Journal* today, I relive with him his experience of that Christmas Eve:

December 25, 1993
Christmas.
A dark night. The morning Star lights up each face. We
   are all alive.
And the light shines in the darkness, and the darkness
   does not overcome it.
It is enough to stand firm in the power of becoming
   children of God,
born here of God.
What has happened to us?
You, the one who is above all,
the unexpected one, who reveals our thirst to us:
   come, oh!
Behold, I come quickly.
We are caught up in the Coming. It remains for us to
   follow the flow of grace.

And a few days later, the last day of this year of 1993, Christopher writes :

December 31, 1993
In your hands, Mary
In your hands, Church of Algeria
I give myself to Crucified love
that he may profess me
as his well-beloved
consecrated in your
I am
the Way, Truth, Life

On January 15, Christopher asked himself a key question and replied with a commentary on the *Rule of Saint Benedict*:

January 15, 1994
15th
Where is fidelity? Who is the one who obeys? The one
    who says and declares categorically and sure of
    himself, "I will never leave this place"?
Or the other one who says, "I would like to go," but
who is still here,
        persevering in your teaching (the Gospel
            here today
        in the monastery until death
        (which came close and is still threatening)
    sharing in your sufferings, oh Christ our Passover,
    by patience
        in order to merit
    to be in your kingdom
        "consortes"
        new Eucharists
        other Christs.

In the monastery until death? Yes, if and as you wish, but not apart from a living fidelity to your teaching, that is, to what the Spirit is saying at this time in the Church.

The next day he continued his meditation:

January 16, 1994
Sunday
In the night, I rendered on your behalf the infinite
service of saying to myself, "I forgive you."
Is it that I know that my body is for you
　　and you for my body?
I cannot say whether I am united with you, I simply
weep and beg never to be separated from you,
　　the temple of your Breath in me
　　that comes from the Father and is given by you.
　　　　I do not belong to myself. Mary is in me as
　　　　the guarantee of that detachment which in
　　　　her was total and radical. Close to her, I am.
　　　　Then I shall be able to glorify you by my
　　　　body.

Christian, with whom I had a long meeting this morning,
tells me of his refusal to imagine his death being imputed
to those he loves here. He remembers the prayer of Brother
Luke during a Mass: "Lord, grant that I may be able to
die without hatred in my heart." There was also S.P. taking to himself the words of Jesus, "No one takes my life,
but it is I who give it." And the phrase of R.Q.: "Three
minutes to say Yes."

I went to talk with Christian about what happened on
the evening of the twenty-fourth, which I experienced as
first a flight, then a waiting, then a coming up from the
abyss.

Where have you led me? Perhaps for myself, it is to
accept continuing to live.
　But could you ask me to accept the death
　　of my brothers?

3
Christmas Eve 1993

From Birth to Birth

Now Fathers Jean-Pierre and Amadeus take up the story. I alternate their reports here, for the sake of easier reading. Only a few details are omitted. The months and years that have passed enable them to be more objective, without taking away the emotions aroused by what they experienced.

(Report of Father Jean-Pierre)

Most Reverend and dear Father,

In this letter I send you my narrative of the visit of Sayat-Attya and his group to Tibhirine on December 24, 1993. It is as I experienced it and remember it. This event marked a turning point in our community life. It is well expressed in the following poem of Brother Christopher:

Returning from work
In front of the red tractor and its noisy weariness,
When the first Door opened
I committed myself
    confident in the openness offered in your faith.
I entered into the peace of your smile
and I loved the glory of the Word on your face.
It is so beautiful, it is so simple,
    it is you who have spoken:
"It is like this in the heart,
That is to say, we must open the doors very wide."

Marvelling, I contemplated the Gospel of God.
The book between us was wide open.
When the second Door opened,
first of all I trembled before this infinity so close,

accessible and poor as a stable.
Showing me the inside of the house,
you let me into the secret,
   this wound towards the inside.
Inviting me to enter further in, you were offering me
   the asylum of a Kingdom.
The future between us is a great open silence.

Excuse me, Father, I had to write everything. I could not stop halfway. This poem expresses so many things, especially when you reread it after the events. I didn't know about its existence. It is the first time I have read it. But you could say that when he wrote it Christopher was already announcing what would happen to him. There are these mysterious Doors written with a capital D. They follow each other chronologically as two passages opening onto the future. There is the verb, "tremble," which describes a first reaction, followed immediately by another one of complete willingness and offering. This is very beautiful and says many things to me. There is the ending: "Inviting me to enter further in, you were offering me the asylum of a Kingdom." This is what happened. He sees it, he has now entered in. "The future between us is a great open silence."

I embrace you, Father.

Brother Jean-Pierre

Context

The GIA group of Muslim fundamentalists had announced that by December 1, 1993 all foreigners should have left the country, or else they would be put to death. Twelve Croatians had just had their throats slit at their work encampment in the neighboring village of Tamesguida. This took place on December 14 towards 10:30 at night. Their throats were slit because they were Christians, in revenge for the Muslims mistreated in Bosnia. The *Testament* of Christian is situated in this context, since it was begun on December 1, 1993 and finished on January 1, 1994. He describes very well the state of mind in which we found ourselves at that time: the uncertainty, the apprehension, a certain anxiety. What is going to happen? "It could be today," says Christian in his *Testament*. We knew that the mountain men were not far away and could raid us at any moment.

December 24, 1993, about 7:00 p.m.

The monks had just gone to bed after the Angelus. Compline is not celebrated this evening, because Christmas Vigils is anticipated at 10:45 P.M. In the guest house, a group of three or four African students from the Center of Administrative Formation (C.F.A.) of Medea, had arrived with R.Q. to participate at the Midnight Mass. Brother Paul, guest master at that time, was with them in the guest house refectory.

I myself, as sacristan, was occupied in the sacristy preparing for Christmas Vigils and Midnight Mass, while Father Celestine, who was preparing the singing, was busy at the bulletin board, at the end of the cloister near the chapel and the small door which opens onto the cloister garden. At the other end of the cloister garden is the entrance door of the monastery.

Through the open door of the sacristy, I hear a rapid, continuous whispering by Celestine. I think to myself, "Who is he talking to?" After a time I hear someone calling me by name from the cloister, "Jean-Pierre, come here!" I turn around and see by the door, a young man in military uniform with a kalachnikov rifle in his hand. He was standing there with Brother Celestine. I understood the situation, went towards him and asked, "What's going on?"

This man had come in by the gate, seen light on the opposite side, crossed the cloister garden and seen Brother Celestine near the bulletin board. How had Celestine reacted? He must have been scared to find himself suddenly in the presence of an armed man, and begun to speak in a low voice. When I asked, "What's going on?" the man, who couldn't have known much French, didn't answer me. He was mainly interested in Brother Celestine. I retraced my steps to get on with my work. Then I carried the tray with the cloths, chalice and cruets in the direction of the chapel to prepare the altar. The man called out, "Come here!" I told myself that we had to obey, thinking he might well begin to shoot. I put down the tray and went towards him.

(Report of Father Amadeus)

After the evening Angelus which Brother Michael has just rung, I leave the chapel and go to the kitchen where I am in the habit of preparing each evening a good, hot herb tea of lime blossoms, picked from our own trees, to help me get to sleep. It is about 7:45 P.M. when I come out of the kitchen to go to my room through the cloister. My room is situated near that of Brother Luke, in the large hall where he stores his many medicines in big, white plastic boxes.

Entering the cloister, near the small refectory bell, I suddenly notice Father Celestine behind a well-dressed armed soldier, preceded by Brother Paul, all of them moving towards the gate to go out. I go up to them and ask Father Celestine in a low voice what this police officer wants. He answers, "You haven't seen them. It's those men from the mountain." Then this man from the mountain turns around and says to me, "Everyone to the guest house!"

Brother Paul, who is walking in front of me then says: "Where's Father Superior? They want to see him." Without stopping to think, I say that he is already in the guest house. When we come to the courtyard of the porter's room, the "mountain man" takes me by the sleeve to drag me along. Sensing the tragedy that could result from having us all assemble in the guest house, I am firmly resolved not to go there. So I pretend to go with him, and then suddenly go to close the entrance door of the monastery which is still wide open. No doubt those lying in wait outside are not far away, but there is no reaction.

I make a half turn and reenter the cloister by the big iron gate near the porter's room, which I close. Turning around, I come face to face with Father Christian. I immediately tell him that an armed group is waiting for him in the guest house. "I know," he says. "I'm in no hurry." He must have been thinking of the first part of his *Testament* written on December 1 in Algiers at the Maison St-Augustin, while waiting to come and pick me up at the airport that evening. It was the very day on which the ultimatum of the GIA expired, making all foreigners in Algeria death targets from that day on. We both returned to Tibhirine, at the mercy of the first ambush! Nothing happened. Christian had already written in that first part of his *Testament*:

> If it should happen one day—and it could be today— that...my life was given to God and to this country...I should like, when the time comes, to have a moment of spiritual clarity which would allow me to beg forgiveness of God and of my fellow human beings.

So Christian walked slowly towards the guest house. I close the gate again, leaving only a tiny chink through which I could see what was happening. All the lights were out except those in the guest house and the lamp at the entrance to the chapel.

Soon I see Father Christian returning, accompanied by a "mountaineer" (*Djebelli*, whom our neighbors call "mountain people"). They are talking in an undertone without raising their voices. They pause a moment in front of the stone statue of our Lady which is at the entrance to our chapel. It came originally from the Visitation Convent of rue du Bac in Paris and was brought here from Staouéli.

I can see the two figures well. They continue to speak for a long time, motionless except for the hands of the man which in the semi-darkness speak as much as his mouth does, as is the Arab-Berber custom with its use of gestures. I did not know at that time that this was the terrible chief of the region, Sayat-Attya, who had presumably given the order, a few days before, to slit the throats of our Croatian brothers. I even heard their conversation, without understanding it. I wait anxiously. Finally the *Djebelli* end by leaving quietly after having rounded up the two others who were in the guest house.

(Report of Father Jean-Pierre)

Brother Michael, who was in the kitchen preparing the hot drink for the guests after Midnight Mass, arrived in the cloister and was invited to follow the man who led us in the direction of the porter's room. We didn't know what to think. Or rather, without admitting it, each one must have thought, "Our turn has come!" When we had reached the courtyard of the porter's room, Brother Paul crossed in front of us, running. He came from the guest house where an armed group had entered and were demanding to see the superior. Brother Paul went to look for Christian who was in his room. We then rejoined the group who were standing at the entrance to the guest house.

There was R.Q., the Africans, and two armed men, one of whom was wearing a turban. This was Sayat-Attya. We did not know this at the time, but we had no doubt that these were the terrorists who had slit the Croatians' throats.

ARRIVAL OF CHRISTIAN

When he arrives, Christian cries out, "This is a house of peace. No one has ever come in here carrying weapons. If you want to talk with us, come in, but leave your arms outside. If you can not do that, we will talk outside." The chief draws Christian apart, halfway between the guest house building and the small gate of the courtyard which opens onto the road. There they had a discussion, in the course of which Sayat-Attya tried to impose several conditions, of which Christian gave us the details later.

During this time, we were talking with the other two "mountaineers," who were standing in the recess of the guest house door. It was chiefly R.Q. who spoke with them, since he knows Arabic well. The subject of the encounter, by and large, was this: "We do not want this government. It is corrupt and irreligious. We must set up an Islamic government. You are religious people, have no fear, we will not harm you."

Our novice, Brother P., who witnesses the scene from the kitchen passage, runs for safety, meets Father Christopher and drags him off to go together and hide in a large tank in the cellar next to the manhole.

Christian's conversation lasted about a quarter of an hour. During this time it seems that another group of three men were on patrol outside in the street. They would have had contact with some local youths who were there. The working classes at that time were on the whole favorable to the mountain people. When the chief's interview with Christian was over, they shook hands with us and withdrew. Certain ones among us felt uncomfortable, thinking that those hands were perhaps the ones that had cut the throats of our Croatian brothers.

WHAT NEXT?

We had had a narrow escape. Brother Luke was sleeping peacefully in his room, not worrying about a thing. So was another priest who had come to spend the night with us. He did not suspect a anything. R.Q. and Christian had a long talk in Christian's office. As for me, I went back to my preparations in the sacristy and chapel. Michael and Celestine, of course, also returned to their work. The two brothers coming out of their tank in the cellar, no longer hearing anything, expected to find us all with our throats cut. The Christmas night liturgy took place at the time and in the way that had been planned. But the atmosphere of prayer could not have been more deeply influenced by what had just occurred.

THE PURPOSE OF THE VISIT

As Christian explained to us after his interview with the chief, the purpose of this unexpected visit appears in the three conditions which the chief required of us:

1. "You are rich," he says. "You must agree to give us money when we ask for it."

2. Your doctor must come and care for our wounded and sick.

3. You must give us medicines. You are religious people, so you must help us in our struggle to set up an Islamic government. You will have to carry out what we

demand of you. You have no choice.

To this Christian had replied, "We are not rich. We work to earn our daily bread. We help the poor. As for sending Brother Luke into the mountains, it is not possible because of his old age and, above all, because of his asthma. He will be able to care for the wounded and sick who come to the dispensary. There is no problem with that. He cares without discrimination for all those in need and does not worry about who they are. As for medicines, he gives what is necessary to every sick person."

Then Christian pointed out to this *Emir* that we were preparing to celebrate the birth of Christ, the feast of Christmas. "In that case," he replied, "please excuse us. We did not know." As he was departing he left a password, since he said, "We shall return."

(Report by Father Amadeus)

Father Christian returned to his office, followed by R.Q. who happened to be in the guest house with three African students from the Center of Administrative Formation, near Medea. They had come to participate in the concelebration of our Midnight Mass. Father Christian and R.Q. begin to comment on the event. I hear them and begin to understand the reasons behind the actions of the *Djebelli*, who the chief is and the nature of his demands as embodied in his phrase, "You have no choice." I see why he stayed outside so as not to enter armed into the guest house, since Father Christian had refused to let him. Meanwhile, another *Djebelli* was talking with R.Q. in the passage.

That was when Father Celestine, very upset, also comes into the superior's office. He tells us that he had had a gun pointed at him as he was on his knees getting out the music sheets from the little cupboard at the entrance to the chapel by the cloister. Then he had been made to go forward on his knees until this "mountain man," the most threatening one of them all, allowed him to rise. Celestine thought his last hour had come.

Knowing almost everything now, I return to my room. Passing in front of Brother Luke's room, I gently knock on his door. He is awake, but tired by all the attention he has given to the sick during the previous day. His voice is gruff as he answers, "What is it?" I enter his room quietly and tell him about this disturbing visit, which has just ended without fuss. The pitiless chief, Sayat-Attya, had excused himself after he learned from Father Christian in the courtyard that he had come on the very night of Christmas when we were about to celebrate the birth of Jesus, son of Mary, prince of peace. But he had said, "We shall return. Give me a password for myself or my envoy." In the face of Father Christian's hesitation, he had said, "All right, it will be 'Monsieur Christian.'" Then, gathering his men, two inside, three outside, they had departed. As always, Brother Luke shrugged his shoulders, not in the least disturbed, at least exteriorly! I retired to my room beside his, to wait for vigils. It was almost 10:00 P.M., but I could not sleep.

At 10:30, Father Christian rings the rising bell. Hearing the bells, Brother P. and Father Christopher, who believed, as they told us later, that we had all had our throats cut, come out from their hiding place and rejoin us in the chapel. At 10:45, entrusting ourselves to the divine Infant whose feast we are keeping and to Mary, his Mother and ours, we sing vigils.

(Report by Father Jean-Pierre)

CONSEQUENCES OF THIS VISIT FOR THE COMMUNITY

The first consequence was obviously that, from one day to the next, we were expecting them again, with their demands. After their visit, we decided not to take any part whatsoever in their cause, which had nothing to do with our monastic vocation, nor with our reason for being in Algeria. If they should one day come to hold us for ransom, we would give them a token sum to free ourselves temporarily from their begging, and leave the monastery immediately. We planned how to react in the case of a rapid departure without any warning, how to know whether or not to take security measures, and what our meeting place would be in case of departure.

We decided to reduce the number of religious for the time being. Two were sent to France to visit their families and P., who was a student, was sent to Algiers. Quite quickly we organized our projects, grouping together several options that had been considered separately at an earlier time. One was that our vow of stability should keep us together for better or worse. More than simply in one place, it united us one to another in such a way that, if we should have to flee, we would reassemble somewhere else with the intention of pursuing there our common vocation together, giving priority to presence among the Muslims. In the second place, this same vow takes on more and more the sign of a visible link with the Church of Algeria in its time of trial and with our Algerian neighbors. Our Lord and Master, from whom we have received our mission in this place, is the one to whom our vow of obedience binds us. We weren't obliged by the orders of the GIA. So long as the neighboring people do not make us feel their desire to have us leave, we will remain with them as in a covenant of love, sharing their difficult situation and trying to bear it with them. The choice to remain unarmed and unprotected by any armed security measures, or by fleeing to the town, was made early in the process, as was a shared decision to follow the gospel "as lambs in the midst of wolves," our only arms being fidelity in charity, and faith in the power of the Holy Spirit working in human hearts. Faith also in the good will of the people, who would hopefully see the trust we had placed in them by leaving ourselves unarmed, in their hands and in such a dangerous spot. It is something of all this that we tried to achieve between ourselves and our neighbors during 1994 and 1995. However, a growing sense of danger hovered over us like a threatening shadow. There was never the least warning sign in spite of other visits requesting help, especially to Brother Luke's dispensary. The danger swooped down on us suddenly and unexpectedly, with nothing which could have let us foresee it. *In manus tuas Domine.*

And so we arrive at January 21, 1994. Four days had passed since I received the large envelope from Algeria. I replied to Christian's letter without delay in order to come close to the community of Atlas. It had been wounded in its life, but only for a greater and better life.

Dear Dom Christian,

Since receiving the chronicle of the events experienced at Atlas in December and the beginning of January, and after our telephone conversation, I want to tell you that you are very such present in our thoughts and prayer, you and your brothers of Atlas.

I have shared what has happened to you with the members of the community of the Generalate. You know almost all of them and so can be assured of their fraternal support and their prayer.

It is not difficult to believe, as you wrote in the chronicle, that in community you have lived through an experience of profound communion, receiving everything moment by moment as a true gift from God. It is still impossible to foresee how events will evolve, but in your manner of living the grace of the present moment, you can be certain that the Lord is with you, fulfilling his word, "I shall be with you until the end of the world, ...for where two or three are gathered in my name, there am I in the midst of them." And, as I said in the homily at the beginning of the General Chapter, he is with you, ready to make use of unexpected means to surmount all obstacles and to work with the grace of salvation in this history which is yours...and ours.

Dear Christian, if I can do anything to help you and your brothers, do not hesitate to let me know and I will do whatever I can to be of service to you.

I embrace you very fraternally...

4
A Visit in Lent

Everything is Easter in the Life of God's Children
The night before Christmas, 1993, as we have just seen, was a "Holy Night," a completely unexpected night for our seven brothers. Much less unexpected, however, was what happened on the Lenten night of Tuesday to Wednesday, March 27, 1996. Toward the end of November 1995, Christian wrote in the name of all the brothers:

The presence of death. Traditionally this is a constant companion of the monk. This companionship has taken on a more concrete clarity with the direct threats we have received, the assassinations very close at hand, and certain visits. It is present to us as a useful test of truth, even though an inconvenient one (Christian, *How We Embody the Charism of our Order in the Present Situation*, November 21, 1995).

On February 27, 1996, one month before the kidnapping, I wrote to Christian and the community for the last time. They never received the letter. I retrieved it during my stay in Algiers and was able to read it with Father Amadeus. I told them:

We shall meet this coming October at the General Chapter, God willing. Meanwhile, I wish you all a fervent preparation for Easter, an Easter already full of the strength and joy of the Resurrection.

At about ten in the morning of that Lenten day, March 26, I arrived with Father André at the monastery of Tilburg, in Holland. The following morning, the twenty-seventh, Dom Armand phoned me from Rome to inform me what had happened the previous night at Tibhirine. At about 2:45 that afternoon, Father André was able to speak on the telephone with Archbishop Teissier of Algiers. A quarter of an hour later, we spoke with Father Jean-Pierre of Atlas. These first reports helped us appreciate immediately the significance of what had happened. At once I shared the reports with Dom Armand and asked him to prepare an urgent report to the presidents of the Regional Conferences, to be communicated to all the monasteries of the order. Thus began a long wait during Lent and Eastertide, which ended shortly before the feast of Pentecost, that is, from March 27 to May 23, 1996. On April 27, exactly one month after the abduction, Communiqué 43 from the GIA was made known. They ask for an exchange of prisoners. The final lines leave little room for hope:

The choice is yours. If you liberate, we shall liberate. If you do not free your prisoners, we will cut the throats of ours.

The Holy Father spoke out during the Palm Sunday Angelus on March 31:

Let them go back to their monastery safe and sound, and let them take up their place again among their Algerian friends.

Two weeks later, during the same prayer to our Lady while he was visiting Tunis, he repeated his plea for setting the monks free. On May 1, feast of Saint Joseph, each and every community of the order dedicated a day to prayer and penance for the freeing of our brothers and for peace in Algeria. Thus we come to May 23. A new communiqué from the GIA ends by saying, "We have cut the throats of the seven monks…. This was done this morning, May 21." You know the rest.

But what exactly happened that Lenten night between March 26 and 27? During my visit to Algiers I had the opportunity to speak about this at length with Fathers Jean-Pierre, Amadeus and L.M. I asked them to be so good as to write down for me all that they experienced in the monastery that night. The three accounts are several pages long. But as the stories are very consistent with one another it is easy to reduce them to a single account. Here is what happened that night of March 26–27 in the words of those who lived through the events. They are not the only witnesses but, as of today, they are the ones who can speak.

(Report of Father Jean-Pierre)

TUESDAY, MARCH 26, 1996—FIFTH WEEK OF LENT.

At the Eucharist, the last Eucharist celebrated together in community, the gospel was John 8:21-30. Jesus announced his departure, "I am going away and you will seek me." To the obstinate Jews, he predicted his death and how it would come about. He also announced, in his death, his exaltation. At the same time he showed his confidence and his inner peace, "He who sent me is always with me, he has not left me alone because I do always the things that please him." The brothers could not have known, on hearing and meditating on these words at that midday hour, that they were about to be taken up, the following night, in the same mystery.

THE NIGHT OF MARCH 26–27, 1996

As I was the night porter, I slept in the porter's room which was immediately next to the porch entrance. This door was bolted shut from 5:30 each evening to 7:30 the next morning. 5:30 in the evening marked the end of the work-day and it was the time we stopped seeing people at the dispensary. That night around 1:15 A.M., I was awakened by the sound of voices near the window of the porter's room which overlooks the yard. It was a conversation in Arabic between two or three persons. Given the hour, I realized immediately that it was a visit from the men of the mountain, who had broken into the cloister. The door-bell had not rung. I got closer to the window to see what was going on, in such a way as not to be seen myself. I could not see the group, since they were in a recess in the doorway, on the right. But a shadowy figure was moving towards them, coming from the small metal door which opens out onto the street. That door was open. The man was armed. He had a submachine gun and was walking towards the others in front of the door. I went to the other side of my room, by the glass door which opens onto the porch entrance to the monastery. I saw a man wearing a turban, with a submachine gun slung across his shoulder, entering the door that opens onto the cloister and to Brother Luke's room. As the conversation and the proceedings did not seem to be aggressive, I did not realize the seriousness of the situation. I thought it was a request for the doctor's care, since this had happened before, in a somewhat similar way. All the more so, because nothing I saw led me to believe that there were around twenty terrorists, as the gatekeeper would later state. The others must have been elsewhere at that point. I told myself that since no one had woken me up, Christian must have beaten me to it and let them in, since the room where he slept was not far from the entrance to the monastery. Actually, according to the gatekeeper, they had gained access to the inside of the monastery not by the main door, but by a door behind the buildings on the basement level, that opens onto the garden. They had therefore arrived at the rooms of Christian and of Brother Luke by passing through the interior of the buildings. At the time I woke up, both of them were already in front of the entrance, in this group in conversation. Christian was in the middle of the courtyard. Brother Luke had in his hand the medical bag he takes on visits. The latter was ready to accompany the men and go to help those who were allegedly seriously wounded. The gatekeeper was also there. It was he who gave me these last details. I began to pray, while waiting for it to end.

At a given moment, I heard someone ask, "Who is the chief?" The reply came from a third person, "He is the chief, you must do what he tells you." At that moment, according to the gatekeeper, the order was given to open all the doors. I heard comings and goings in the entrance hall, but only of isolated individuals. Then, nothing more. The small door opening onto the street was closed with its characteristic sound. I went out to go to the bathroom before going back to bed. The cloister lights had been extinguished (by Father Amadeus, as it turns out). Everything seemed to me to be in order. I thought that Christian had sent the men of the mountain away and had returned to bed. One thing seemed strange, however: some of the type of clothing that Brother Luke used to collect for the poor was strewn on the ground under the porch and in the adjoining room. I said to myself, "Did they ask for some clothing, which they didn't like and threw there on their way out?" A few minutes later, there was a knock at my door, the glass door which opens onto the porch. It was Father Amadeus accompanied by L.M. "Do you know what has happened?" he asked. "We are the only ones here. All the others have been taken away."

(Report by Brother Amadeus)

It was 1:15 in the early morning of Wednesday, March 27, 1996, when I was awakened by the unusual sound of cartons of medicines being noisily turned upside down. I said to myself, "When Brother Luke is looking for medicine, even at night, he doesn't make this much noise." Then I heard some speaking in a low tone of voice near my room, but I did not hear Brother Luke's voice, nor his asthmatic cough. I suddenly realized that they were there, that they had come in the middle of the night. I had had no illusions about what was taking place! We had not received any threats since the famous night of Christmas 1993, when the terrible leader had left in apologies, awed by the birth of Jesus bringing peace, as Father Christian had explained to him. But he said he would return, and that we had no choice. He had not returned, either to require that the young people of the neighborhood join their group, nor to ambush and kill persons on the road to Tibhirine. Father Jean-Pierre, Father R. and Brother Luke often travelled that road to do their errands. And so we had been able to continue our monastic life in a normal way these three years, even to the point of authorizing the dialogue group, *Ribât es-Salâm*, to meet at our monastery on the very eve of the tragedy.

And so this commando group of about twenty terrorists, sent from afar, under orders, was there, two steps away from my room. They had tried to open it. Every night I took the trouble to lock the door. Probably concerned with the boxes of medicines in the main room, they did not keep trying to open my door for the moment. I looked at my watch with a small covered light. It was 1:15. I dressed silently. I tried to see through the keyhole. The room was completely lit up. They continued to overturn boxes of medicines, but they were too close to Brother Luke's room for me to see them. They continued to speak softly among themselves.

I waited calmly. Suddenly there was no more noise, but all the lights had been left on. I gently opened my door without making any noise. I could see that no one was around, but everything in the room was in great disorder. I went immediately to Brother Luke's room a few steps away from mine. There was no longer anyone there and the room was in great disorder. Medicines and books were on the floor. The little new radio set had disappeared. Sensing the tragedy that had taken place, I went immediately to Father Christian's office where he had been sleeping for some time, in order to be near us. It was just opposite the door which opens from Brother Luke's room onto the little scriptorium corridor. The office was open and all lit up, everything upside down, papers everywhere. His electric typewriter was gone, as was the camera with the film already begun. The telephone had been taken from the table, with all wires cut and left on a chair. No Brother Luke, no Father Christian, no voices, not even Brother Luke's cough. I was aghast. Some of Father Christian's clothes and shoes had been taken and then discarded in the corner of the corridor.

I soon began to think of our guests of the *Ribât*, on the same floor, near the rooms of our brothers. I extinguished all the lights and went up the stairs near the library. The rooms of the brothers were open and the lights were on, but none of my brothers were there and their beds were left unmade. The floor was covered with papers. Drawers had been emptied. Suitcases had been opened. And no one was there! It was a shock. I began to fear the worst for our guests who slept just behind the enclosure door. I opened it gently and there everything was calm. The night light was on, the bedroom doors shut. I knock at the first door, the cell where L.M. slept.

(Report from L.M., a guest)

C.M., a priest and member of our *Ribât*, woke me up, saying, "L.M., something strange is happening with the fathers." I leap out of bed and go out into the hallway. Another priest, D.X., and I were sleeping in the guest rooms of the monastic buildings, separated by just a doorway from the rooms of the monks. I listen and hear tables and chairs being moved around, but no voices except for some protests that seem to come from Celestine. So I assume he is sick and that they want to move him down near Brother Luke, since they don't want to take him to the hospital at night.

C.M. half opens the door to the monks' enclosure and sees the gate keeper with his back to the wall, perfectly still between the two doors. Celestine is also perfectly still, and there is a suitcase in the hallway. The gate keeper eventually notices that our door is ajar and signals with his head not to enter or move. When C.M. tells us this, we realize that the "people from the mountain" are in the monastery and I suppose that the monks have been forced to assemble together. C.M. half opens the door again. There is now only the suitcase in the hallway. Then silence.

C.M. half opens the door again. The suitcase is no longer there.

There is no question of making ourselves conspicuous, or of leaving by the outside staircase, since there are probably armed men all around the building. Each guest goes back to his room in silence. If we are involved in what is going on, Christian will come to tell us. I thought that the moment of death had arrived. I went back to bed. I was cold but I was very calm, asking the Lord to hold me in his peace. At the same time, I ask him to postpone the day of my passing away, because so many administrative affairs are in process that I fear the enormous task the diocese would have if I should disappear without first putting some of my affairs in order. I was also listening for exterior noises, or the engine of a car. At that moment, the door opens, a lamp lights up my room and by the light of the night light in the hall, I recognize Brother Amadeus. He says, "L.M., are you there? The monastery is empty. There isn't a single father left!"

I dress in great haste and I see with Amadeus that the rooms of the brethren are all in disorder. In Paul's, who returned from France just yesterday and brought back gifts for Easter, all the boxes of candy and chocolates have been opened and emptied, except one. Perhaps they thought those chocolates contained alcohol. I later returned to get this box and put it in the refrigerator for when the brothers came back. The candy wrappings were strewn on the floor. Surprisingly, the computer and printer had been left. We went downstairs to the kitchen. Everything was in place except that the door of the refrigerator had been left open. Nothing had been touched in the refectory.

 In the cloister, the room that served as an office and telephone room had not been opened. Everything was in place. But the telephone lines had been cut. We went towards the porter's room. The main doorway was open. We knocked at Jean-Pierre's door. "It's Amadeus, are you there?" Jean-Pierre opened the door, fully dressed. He had been praying. What a joy to finding him! We told him of the disappearance of the monks. He told us he saw armed men on the porch and that he heard them leave, but had not seen the brothers with them.

(Father Jean-Pierre)

We went to examine the state of the rooms, Christian's room as well as Brother Luke's. Everything was in indescribable disorder: papers on the floor, drawers emptied, cupboards open, tables piled with different objects, Christian's typewriter gone, also his camera. Our first thought was to bring in the security service, but we found that Christian's telephone cables had been cut. In the secretary's office, all was in order. They must not have gone there, but that telephone was not working either. Later that day we found out that the outside cables had been cut. The one that connected the monastery with the guardian's house was on the ground. Even the main cable which contained the lines of that whole area had been cut about a mile away on the road to Medea. Clearly, it was something very different from just wounded persons who needed to be treated. In the rooms on the floor of the secretary's office, that is, the cells of Christopher, Paul, Bruno, Michael, and Celestine, there was the same disorder. Paul had just returned the evening before from a visit to his elderly mother in Savoy. His suitcase had been searched and certain objects had disappeared. In the hallway of the reading room, at the foot of the stairs, Amadeus sees a large cheese from Tamié, placed in front of the icon of the Mother of the Lord. It hadn't been taken on account of the cross on the wrapping. We didn't find anyone's identity papers, except those of Christian in a little bag which we discovered later in one of the files, and Brother Luke's, also found later among his things. According to the gatekeeper, the kidnappers would have ordered the brothers to take all their papers. Apart from the rooms on that floor, Brother Luke's room and the room where his medicines were stored, and Father Christian's room, none of the other parts of the monastery seem to have been visited. The departure of the brothers seems to have been very hurried. Which way did they go? I don't know. I saw nothing, nor did I hear a group of people leaving, nor any voice that I could have recognized, such as Brother Luke's strong voice or his way of coughing. Nothing. If I had realized that they were taking the brothers away, what would I have done?

(L.M.)

We needed to inform others at once, so we went to the gatekeeper's house to telephone. There was a padlock on the door to the courtyard of his house. We called. Finally his children, then his wife, came to tell us, "They came to look for him." Their telephone line had also been cut.

(Father Jean-Pierre)

We found his wife panic-stricken. It was then that we learned that the kidnappers had begun by contacting the gatekeeper at his home. They had forced him to open the entrance by knocking on the door and breaking windows, and then to accompany them to the monastery, saying that they needed to call Brother Luke and get him to accompany them to treat two seriously wounded persons. At that, we thought that the gatekeeper must have been taken away with our brothers, since we didn't see him. I stayed for a short time with his wife and children to comfort them and help them cope while waiting for more news.

(L.M.)

We needed to inform other neighbors and to try to telephone. Jean-Pierre and I each took a flashlight and went down to A.'s, lighting only the path by our feet, so we could find the way to his house, which was not easy since it is situated down from the road. At the same time I felt anxious, and wanted to return to the monastery, while feeling the need to tell A.what had happened. Finally I found the door. No one answered. I went up to the terrace, tapping with my foot. No one budged. It was only then that the dogs awoke and began to bark. As no one came out—and that was perfectly understandable—we went back to the monastery.

It was nearly three in the morning. With Amadeus, D.X., and C.M., we decided to wait until daybreak. To have left by car for Medea in the night risked adding another victim and having the car stolen as well. To have gone on foot to alert the police was to risk their not answering. We decided to go back to bed, but Amadeus told us, "I haven't finished my rosary," a rosary he was reciting while Jean-Pierre and I were out in the night. We recited the rest of the rosary with Amadeus and we arranged to rise at 5:00 A.M. I had a deep peace in my heart, with the sense that there was nothing else to do at that point. At 5:15 we met in the cloister, C.M., Jean-Pierre, and Amadeus. I had the urge to ring the bell for matins to show everyone that life continued, but I changed my mind, thinking that it could also inform the kidnappers that they hadn't taken all the monks. We began the Office. I felt honored to hold the place in choir of the abducted brothers, as best I could. At the end of the second psalm, C.M. and I could no longer follow the monastic tones and we decided to recite the psalms. After the Office, we ate a good breakfast.

It was daybreak. Jean-Pierre and I went down to A.'s house again. I went back up on the terrace, called and kicked with my feet again. The children finally came out of the house to tell us what had happened. At that point, the gatekeeper called out to me from the other side of the fence. He was in the garden. He had escaped and had hidden himself. He immediately asked news of his family and the brothers. We went to get him. He was exhausted. He told us what he had experienced and how he had escaped.

We urgently needed to inform the army and the police. I decided to go with Jean-Pierre and leave the gatekeeper to rest a little. I feared the interrogation that he would have to undergo from the police. Jean-Pierre proposed that we first go to see the head of the military station, whom he knew personally. Jean-Pierre and I took my car and drove towards Draa-ess-Mar to inform the military. There was a thick fog. On the way, we decided not to delay but to go straight to Medea to inform the police. We arrived at 7:15. The police commander was just leaving with three cars for a planned operation. He received us immediately but showed neither surprise nor emotion at what we told him. Everything was explained in Arabic. He immediately phoned the chief of police, and he authorized me to inform Archbishop Teissier. He let me use his phone. The archbishop asked me if he might inform the French ambassador. I passed on the request to the commander who, after a moment's hesitation, gave his permission. The police would themselves inform the Algerian Press Service, who would announce the news that morning. I was most surprised at this exceptional speed. But the commander had to leave on business. He handed us over to an assistant. They bring us coffee. We wait. There are no more cars available to provide a convoy to Tibhirine.

At about nine o'clock, an officer comes to take our statement. Everything is in Arabic. I serve as translator. I make them read over the statements before we sign them. The police hold a dossier with all the information on the French monks. Amadeus, being an Algerian, is not included. We had to find Bruno in a previous dossier. At 11:00, they finally allow us all to leave. All the police we had met had been friendly and attentive. Only one of them spoke French. Many of them seemed quite familiar with the texts of Islam, but had little knowledge of other religions. They apologized to us. On the return trip we notice that a team from the telephone company is repairing the telephone cable that had been severed on top of the hill at the same level as the entrance to the former amusement park.

When we arrived at the monastery, we saw that all the members of the *Ribât* had left for Algiers except C.M., who had not wanted to leave Brother Amadeus alone in the monastery. I decided to stay with Amadeus and Jean-Pierre as long as necessary. C.M. felt that he should join the group in Algiers and Jean-Pierre remembered the car of Father V.L., who was not now in Algiers and had left his car at the monastery. So C.M. left for Algiers in that car, which would be safer at the chancery. A first group of police had come at about 10:00 A.M. to verify what had happened. But all that day we saw no movement of troops in that region. The neighbors were not interrogated. At noon it was time to celebrate Mass and sing sext. It was an intense celebration. Amadeus and Jean-Pierre asked me to preside. A deep peace filled me, as well as joy at sharing this day with the two brother monks. I felt I was in my place at that point. There was an astonishing presence of our missing brothers in that empty chapel.

(Father Jean-Pierre)

Towards noon, the three of us celebrated the Eucharist in the monastery chapel. L.M. presided. He commented on the texts of the Wednesday of the fifth week of Lent in connection with what had taken place. The passage from Daniel related the incident of the three youths in the furnace and really spoke to us. They preferred to be thrown into the furnace rather than obey the king's orders and adore false gods. Although bound, they found themselves free, unharmed in the midst of the flames, praising God with a single heart. Their courage and fidelity towards God, and the powerful intervention of the Lord, brought about a radical change in the heart of the king. He also began to praise God, the God of Shadrach, Meshach and Abednego.

(L.M.)

Amadeus and Jean-Pierre confided to me that they did not know how to cook, so I was happy to prepare the meal. The telephone, once reconnected, did not stop ringing. The first call came from a cousin of Brother Luke who asked for news, because his brother, who was in Zaire, had informed him of the abduction of the monks! Then there was the annoying insistence of the newspaper reporters. I refused to talk to them. We eventually had our lunch. While doing the dishes, we received a call from Christian's mother and sister, Madame de Chergé and Claire. They were concerned about the safety of the monks remaining on the property, asking how they were and encouraging them.

We realized that the two large pots in the kitchen were full, one with soup and the other with beans. Luke had prepared the meal for the whole household in the middle of the night, as he often did, just before he was abducted.

There was soup and beans for nine monks and twelve members of the *Ribât*. We decided to rest until none. When we finished the Office a police squadron arrived to make an inquiry and take photos. We had not touched anything until their arrival. The police were surprised by the monks' simplicity of life. With them was a detachment of armed men. I remembered Christian's attitude on the night of the visit of December 24, 1993, and I asked the armed men to leave the cloister and wait outside: "This is a house of peace and prayer. No armed men enter here." They went out without the least opposition. Then the one in charge of security asked us not to spend the night in the place. We proposed sleeping at R.Q.'s, who left his keys in the monastery. He telephones us from Paris soon after, to give us details. The police wish to accompany us before nightfall and we agree with them to leave at 7:00 P.M. At this moment a neighbor arrives with a cowl which he found on the road a third of a mile from the monastery. It is Michael's. I imagine Michael taking his cowl so that he can die in his habit. Amadeus, Jean-Pierre and I begin to put the brothers' rooms in order. We look for their identity papers, without success, and realized that each of them had taken the small suitcase that he had kept in readiness. The gatekeeper tells us that the armed men had ordered the brothers to take their papers.

I block all the entrances to the monastery with thick wooden planks. We sing vespers. We eat the soup and beans prepared by Luke with a salad from the garden. We take what we need for the night along with a suitcase full of precious objects and the money. Between two police cars, we left for Medea. As we approached the Grand Hotel Msala, the first car turned to enter the hotel grounds. I continued towards R.Q.'s house but the car behind signaled me to stop. They wanted us to go to the hotel. The police lieutenant explained that the *Wali* had reserved rooms for us there. And so the three of us entered this large hotel, carrying our bed linen in our arms, and were welcomed in the grandest style. They invited us to dine in the restaurant. We excused ourselves, as we had already dined. They invited us to have coffee. It was a delightful and touching sight to see our two brothers in their jackets and woolen hats, sitting at table in the restaurant, surrounded by the proprietor of the hotel, the police chief, the head of the *Wali*'s cabinet and the chief of security of the *Wilaya*, who had come to welcome them. All the people who saw us were astounded.

We went up to our rooms: two rooms, each with two beds and a bathroom. There was a communicating door between the rooms. A detachment of security guards was placed in front of the doors. We arranged to meet the police the following morning at eight o'clock. We sang compline and went to bed. I asked the brothers to excuse me from rising for the night office. In the morning, after singing lauds, we go down to breakfast. The police are there, we return to the monastery. I make arrangements for the day with the police lieutenant. We will leave for Algiers about 4:00 P.M. In the morning, Amadeus has errands to carry out in Medea. I act as his chauffeur and I ask the police lieutenant not to surround us with police vehicles in order not to scare the people of Medea. He agrees to this. Just one car follows us at a distance. We go with Amadeus to get money from the bank, to pay the fuel man who has filled the monastery pumps, and then we return. Everywhere we are welcomed warmly, but with much sadness of heart.

At the monastery we decided on what we need to take: the archives, precious objects, electronic devices and perishable food. Amadeus paid the workmen. From the chancery of Algiers, the archbishop suggested some helpers. P.L. and P.R., the hermit, who was absent at the time of the tragedy, will come to help us move. Military guards are posted at the doors of the monastery. I prepare lunch. At 12:30 we celebrate Mass and sext, then sit down to eat when P.L. and P.R. arrive. I closed all the doors so that the military would not wander around in the house. Halfway through the meal, a phone call came from the gatekeeper, "Everything is shut. We can't get in. The archbishop, the French ambassador and the *Wali* are here!" The brothers decide to receive them in the chapter room. I go to open the main door to receive them. Behind the authorities, a crowd of armed men press forward. I stop them in the cloister and explain to them the character of this house. They accept it courteously and retire to the outside gate.

The brothers recount the facts again to the ambassador and the *Wali*. We thank the *Wali* for the protection and for the reception at the hotel. We talk of security measures for the house and promise to leave at 4:00 that afternoon. The brothers are authorized to come back to the monastery during the day. An escort will accompany us all the way to Algiers. When the authorities retire, the archbishop invites the ambassador to visit the chapel with the brothers. I ask the *Wali* if he would like to come into the chapel, too. When he answers in the affirmative, I invite him to come in with me. The police commander wanted to follow us in, but at a sign from my hand he understood very courteously that this would not be appropriate. The same applied to the ambassador's bodyguard.

Our distinguished visitors left us and we had an hour to finish closing up the house and to pack the cars. The brothers left theirs for the use of the gatekeeper, so that he could sleep in Medea. P.R. wanted to remain at the monastery, but I insisted firmly that he should go with us, since I had promised that no one would spend the night in the monastery. At this point, a police officer realized that Amadeus had not been interrogated, because being an Algerian, he was not on the list of foreigners. I insisted that he give a statement, and had the text reread in Arabic before allowing him to sign it. The police officer was astonished that we were leaving everything in place. I told him it was normal, as the fathers would return. We checked to make sure that everything was extinguished and well closed at the guest house and all over the monastery. We loaded the cars and said good-bye to all the neighbors. "Don't leave us," they pleaded, "you must return." A police car preceded us and two armored cars followed our two cars. Arriving in Algiers, I led the convoy and directed it to the chancery, where we arrived around 5:30 P.M.

I am happy to have lived through those two intense days with Amadeus and Jean-Pierre, who remained always serene, peaceful and humble. I am glad to have experienced the strength given from on high to accomplish what needed to be done at the moment without unnecessary fuss, and to have enjoyed the unfolding of a normal monastic day, astonished at having come so close to death and feeling thereby a new freedom. May I spend the time that is left to me in giving thanks!

The Following Weeks

(Father Jean-Pierre)

We stayed at the chancery until the following Saturday, the day when Dom Armand Veilleux arrived on behalf of our Father General. He came to embrace us with all his solicitude and fraternal presence for about ten days, until Thursday, April 11. All three of us then went together to *Les Glycines* where Father Georger gave each of us a room in those calm and silent quarters. Father Amadeus and I waited there, day after day, for news of our dear missing brothers. Towards the end of April, we decided to go to Fes at the beginning of May. At first both of us were to go, but then I alone, because we learned at Tibhirine that P.R. and our neighbors were counting very much on our maintaining a concrete link with them. I left Algeria for Fes on May 3.

The sanctuary lamp in our chapel at Tibhirine was blown out on that sad night of March 26–27. The chapel, that had echoed with the chants and prayers at the regular hours of the Divine Office since 1937, became suddenly silent and empty. "How long, O Lord?" Our hearts reply, "It is only an *au revoir*, until we meet again." "Our brothers have gone away." It was the time just before Holy Week and a great, long trial was in store for them. They completed their course while paschal time was coming to an end, during the week before Pentecost: "Come, O Spirit of the Lord, come, alleluia!" They were calling down the Holy Spirit on the Church and on the world. They were caught up into the Work of God down to the innermost depth of their being, body and soul. Through it, they were heard in their fervent desire to be totally one with him and to follow him wherever he goes. The Lord is magnificent and all my heart sings to God! What will happen to those of us who remain? We shall see!!! I am surprised at the great solidarity aroused on the occasion of this tragedy, a solidarity in emotion, pain and prayer, as well as in hope.

5
Wisdom Comes from Memory

Teachers and Mystics in the School of Charity

Christian wisdom consists in a divine plan of salvation.
This plan has its source and its summit in the paschal mystery of Jesus Christ. That is why Jesus is the "Wisdom of
God" (1 Cor 1:24). To practise wisdom is to remember and
keep in one's heart the saving interventions of God in history, putting into practice the norms of conduct which flow
from them. We invoke Mary, the Mother of Jesus Christ, as
the Seat of Wisdom for two reasons: for having conceived
Incarnate Wisdom in her womb, and for having conceived
in her heart the wisdom that comes from meditating, pon-
dering and interpreting the words and saving deeds of Christ
the Lord.

The Lord has done great things in the life of our brothers.
His work in them is also a word. In these pages we have let
them express their thoughts and feelings. They themselves
have told us their story and have revealed its meaning to
us. It is true: God still reveals his secrets to his friends, the
prophets.

Since their passover, our seven brothers have begun to
work wonders in our order and in the Church. It is the hour
to begin listening to what the Spirit, working in them, is
saying to the Church, to the world and to this school of
schools of charity, which is the Cistercian Order.

1. There is a first series of messages directed to all men and
   women of good will. The hidden, silent passing of these
   brothers is transformed into a Gospel appeal which
   resounds unambiguously:

   i) Ask forgiveness from God for these aggressors. Only
      forgiveness can break the chain of hatred and violence.
      To forgive is an act of profound respect which enables

us to discover in the offender, beyond all dissimilarity, the image of God. To forgive is to acknowledge and proclaim that, despite all our malice and ignorance, God recognizes us as well-beloved sons and daughters. To forgive is to bear witness, in spite of everything, to our condition as children of God and to our common destiny, which is divine. The word which is most in harmony with the heart of the martyr is the word of pardon because that word is a faithful witness to love.

I should like, when the time comes, to have a moment of spiritual clarity which would allow me to beg forgiveness of God and of my fellow human beings, and at the same time to forgive with all my heart the one who will strike me down (Christian, *Testament*).

ii) The martyr who gives up his life while forgiving, does not accuse anyone. An extremist group is not representative of a people. Nothing would be more absurd than to blame the Algerian people or the Islamic world for what has happened. Nor should we accuse the ones who were physically responsible for the tragedy. We should trust that the word of forgiveness is able to dispel all ignorance and malice, allowing the light to grow in oneself and to find spaces of freedom for the transformation of one's own existence. Every human being deserves to be loved.

I do not see, in fact, how I could rejoice if the people I love were indiscriminately accused of my murder. It would be too high a price to pay for what will perhaps be called, the "grace of martyrdom," to owe this to an Algerian, whoever he may be, especially if he says he is acting in fidelity to what he believes to be Islam.... And also you, my last minute friend, who will not have known what you were doing: Yes, I want this THANK YOU *and this "*A-DIEU*" to be for you, too, because in God's face I see* *yours. May we meet again as happy thieves in Paradise, if it please God, the Father of us both.* AMEN! (Christian, *Testament*).

iii) Martyrs of love are true artisans of peace. It is not simply a matter of being patient and putting up with or tolerating evil. Nor is it enough to be peaceful in the sense of not doing or wishing harm to anyone. Much more is needed. Peace can only be constructed by the gift of one's own life. No one took it from them, they gave it up.

I do not think violence can eradicate violence. We can only exist as human beings by accepting to make ourselves the image of Love, as is shown in Christ who, though being himself just, wished to submit himself to the lot of the unjust (Luke, *Letter*, March 24, 1996).

iv) Human life has a meaning. It is a path to a goal. This meaning is only found when life is given gratuitously and offered with a pure heart. If life is a gift that has been received, then whoever converts his life into a gift that is offered, lives and causes others to live. To love is to live. And death can be the final act of love, capable of giving an eternal meaning to life.

There is no true love of God without an unreserved acceptance of death (Luke, *Letter*, March 19, 1995).

2. The Spirit is also speaking today to the Church universal and to all local Churches, in the following terms:

v) The Christian-Muslim interreligious dialogue now has new motives for continuing. Seven lives offered for this dialogue are a good foundation for mutual understanding. They knew that actions speak louder than many words.

Not having the linguistic and religious knowledge necessary to enter into dialogue with Islam, I feel called more simply to listen. It is God who is heard in his Word who is sent. It is he who tells me to listen and to welcome all this strange, different reality, even to the point of feeling myself responsible for it, that the Spirit may lead it towards the full truth. And if we can walk this road together, so much the better! We will be able to speak and to be silent as we walk (Christopher, *Journal,* January 30, 1996).

We have to be witnesses of the Emmanuel, that is, of "God with us." There is a presence of "God among men" which we ourselves must assume. It is in this perspective that we understand our vocation to be a fraternal presence of men and women who share the life of Muslims, of Algerians, in prayer, silence and friendship. Church-Islam relations are still stammering because we have not yet lived side by side with them enough (Christian, *Reflections for Lent,* March 8, 1996).

vi) The seven martyrs of Atlas are a ripe fruit of their local Church and of the Algerian people. They decided to remain in Algeria so that they could continue living to the very end from this Church and for this people. They wished to be the Church in Algeria for the Algerian people.

If something happens to us, though I hope it does not, we want to experience it here, in solidarity with all the Algerian men and women who have already paid with their life, simply in solidarity with all those unknown, innocent people.... It seems to me that He who is helping us to hold fast today is the One who has called us. I remain in deep wonder at this (Michael, *Letter,* April 1994).

I am certain that God loves the Algerians, and that he has chosen to prove it to them by giving them our lives. So then, do we truly love them? Do we love them enough? This is a moment of truth for each one of us, and a heavy responsibility in these times when our friends feel so little loved. Slowly, each one is learning to integrate death into this gift of self and, with death, all the other conditions of this ministry of living together, which is necessary for total selflessness. On certain days, all this appears hardly reasonable: as unreasonable as becoming a monk (Christian, *Circular Letter to the Community*, April 25, 1995).

vii) God uses what is weak to build great things. Only obscure witnesses of a hope can become luminous martyrs of love. They made the choice to be small seeds buried in the ground so that the giant tree of the Kingdom might grow.

In a few months, what will remain of the Church in Algeria, of its visibility, its structures, the persons of whom it is made up? Little, very little, probably. However, I believe that the Good News is sown, the grain is germinating…. The Spirit is at work, he works deep down in the hearts of men. Let us be willing that he be able to work in us by prayer and loving presence to all our brothers (Paul, *Letter*, January 11, 1995).

Our Church has been severely shaken, especially in our diocese of Algiers. Reduced, ravaged, she lives the poignant experience of the renunciation and reward described in the Gospel as belonging to the vocation of all who follow Jesus. Vulnerable, fragile in the extreme, she finds herself also freer and more credible in her vow "to love to the end" (Christian, *How We Embody the Charism of our Order in the Present Situation*, November 25, 1995).

In the face of death, tell me that my faith—which is Love—will hold strong. Suddenly I am terrified to believe (Christopher, *Journal*, February 1, 1994).

Here I am before you, my God…. Here I am, rich in misery and poverty, full of unspeakable cowardice. Here I am before You who are nothing but Mercy and Love. Before you, but solely by your grace, I am here whole and entire, with all my soul, all my heart, all my will (Bruno, March 21, 1990).

3. There is also a word for us, monks and nuns of the Cistercian Order of the Strict Observance. For us who, after nine centuries of existence, are preparing to cross the threshold of a new millennium with hearts renewed and enlarged.

   viii) They followed Jesus to the end, according to the absolute truth of the gospel. They took on the attitudes and choices of Jesus. They embraced his destiny. They were disfigured with him in order to be configured to him. They took on themselves the cross of abnegation in order to hasten the coming of the Kingdom. They preferred nothing to the love of Christ, who is the Servant of the servants of God.

   I ask of you this day the grace to become a servant
   and to give my life
   here
   as a ransom for peace
   as a ransom for life
   Jesus draw me
   into your joy
   of crucified love

   (Christopher, *Journal*, July 25, 1995).

   ix) They were plunged into the mystery until they were completely transformed. A mysterious influence enabled them to experience the mystery to the point of becoming fire and light. Our seven mystics stretch out their hands to introduce us, too, into the transforming glory of God. They invite us to fix our gaze on the obscurity of the darkness until we contemplate the face of the Other. They tell us that there is no transcendence without transparency and immanence. Word and

Eucharist are the door leading into the heart of God, who is the source of all transformation.

You speak to me when I say and sing: "As for me,
*   thanks to your love,*
I have access to your house."
There within myself—so far yet so near.
In you I have access to my I, given up to the love with
*   which you are loved.*
Whoever loves me—and how can I say that I love if not
*   thanks to your very Breath—*
We will come to him,
I and my Father

(Christopher, *Journal*, March 4, 1994).

x) They lived together, died together and entered together into eternal life. The community is the sacred place where God reveals himself. Love welded them together in a bond of everlasting solidarity. Common life is worth very little if there is no communion of life. *Koinonia* makes the Risen One visible. Then he, in turn, makes all things new. Our brothers did not pursue what they judged better for themselves, but instead, what was better for the others. That is why the Lord brought them, all together and at the same time, to everlasting life.

Listen, Church: I am.
Listen, I am in you, as the Father is in me,
*   He in me and I in Him,*
we are ONE
Listen: I am in you the Resurrection, the Life.
Thanks to you (in you, with you),
*   I break through the wall.*
There is my sin standing before me—
*   this lack of oblative love for my*
*   brothers—but thanks to you*
I do not remain frightened or despairing too long....

I break through death.
And so, when my fraternal existence
  will be lived out on the other side,
Since you desire to see us come
  all together to this eternal Life,
You say to me today: Arise, go to yourself,
  to your true Easter I

(Christopher, *Journal*, October 30, 1994).

For the community of Atlas, Christmas 1993 was an experience that marked them for the rest of their lives. Two years later they recognized that

...through that experience we felt invited to be born again. The life of a man goes from birth to birth.... In our life there is always a child to be born: the son of God whom each of us is (Christian, *Reflections for Lent*, March 8, 1996).

We too, Cistercian monks and nuns, are invited by what happened to our brothers to be born again. The path has been marked out, we have only to walk along it.

With Jesus, all together, towards the Father.
From the Order, through the Church, to the whole human race.
Opening ourselves up to inculturation, discernment, ecumenism and dialogue.

It is not a matter of dying, but of living from our roots, from our first Love. If the price of fidelity to this is death, let us pay the price, knowing that this is how Life is purchased.

O Jesus, I accept with all my heart that your death is renewed and fulfilled in me. I know that it is with you that we come back from the frightening descent into the depths, proclaiming to the devil that he has been conquered (Celestine, *Easter antiphon*).

The true pilgrim has his two feet firmly planted in the present and raises them promptly in his journey toward the future, knowing that the Lord is guiding his steps. The road opens before him as he walks, as long as there is music and song in his heart. In a letter which appeared only after his death, Father Celestine himself said it in all simplicity:

> *In carrying out my daily duties—and this helps me each day— I sing two short phrases this morning: "O God, you are our Hope on the face of all the living," and "Wonder of your grace! You entrust to men the secrets of the Father"* (*Letter*, January 22, 1996).

I embrace you fraternally in Mary of Saint Joseph,

Bernardo Olivera
Abbot General

CHAPTER IV
Keeping their Memory Alive

May 21, 1997

Very dear Brothers and Sisters,

Pope John Paul II sent a message to our General Chapters from the Gemelli Hospital last October 10, 1996.* He ended it by saying:

> Brothers and sisters, you are the custodians of this martyrdom, the persons on watch in prayer, in shared discernment and in the concrete directives which you decide upon, so that the memory of this event remain fruitful in the future for Trappists and for the whole Church.

It is true. We are the heirs of the martyrdom suffered by our brothers. We have no doubt that they are the light of the world. A lamp is not lit and then put under a basket. It is set on a lampstand. What, then, can we do to have the memory of these events bear fruit for the order and for the entire Church? The first thing that comes to mind as a reply is to share with each of you, my brothers and sisters, on this first

---

*The Pope's message can be found in Chapter V, page 130.

anniversary of the passage of our brothers, what I consider to be the heart of the heritage they have left us.

My sharing with you is not just on the level of information. It is a question of forming our lives as the Lord formed theirs. So I want to present to you here, with the greatest possible clarity and conviction, the key to interpreting everything they lived through. In his message, the Holy Father told us that

> The *Testament* which Dom Christian de Chergé left behind contains the key for understanding the tragic event in which he and his confreres were involved, the final meaning of which is the gift in Christ of their life. "My life," he wrote, "was given to God and to this country."

So the inner key for understanding our brothers is the commitment of their lives to the following of Jesus. This principle of interpretation lets us enter into the mystery of the community of Our Lady of Atlas. The following of Christ implies a double reality. The first is dynamic, a movement. The second is static, remaining with him. Obviously remaining near Jesus depends on moving toward him. This double reality comes to form a single one made up of the dedication and gift of self. The person given to Jesus moves toward him so as to be transformed by him and in him. Unfortunately, and it is sad to say so, Christian and monastic life is full of persons who are "deeply moved," but hardly move at all.

1
Death and Life
Following Jesus to the Shedding of Blood

Let us review the facts that we already know. It was October 1993. The Armed Islamic Group (GIA) had begun its aggressive action against foreigners living in Algeria. Three foreign consular agents were kidnapped, then set free with the message that all foreigners must leave the country within a month. At the end of this one month period of grace, four foreigners were assassinated by the GIA as a proof that the latter's warnings were to be taken seriously. On December 14, twelve Catholic Croats had their throats slit. The brothers knew them, since they lived in Tamesguida, only a few miles from the monastery. The GIA claimed responsibility for the murders. A few days later, the night of Christmas Eve, our brothers received a visit from the GIA. The guerrillas were looking for financial aid, medical assistance and material supplies. They made an effort to win the monks over to their cause. As they departed they left a promise: "We shall return."

The number of victims and the rhythm of violent incidents increased at a frightening rate. On May 8, 1994, the first official representatives of the Catholic Church in Algeria were killed: a Marist Brother, Henri Vergès, and a Little Sister of the Assumption: Paule Hélène Saint Raymond. Father Christopher of Atlas wrote in his diary:

> This witness to you is given by your servants, both men and women: your friends. It has a long history and goes on, merged with the Eucharist (*Journal*, May 10, 1994).

Two Augustinian sisters, Caridad María Álvarez and Esther Alonso, were assassinated on October 23. The next day Father Christopher commented that the killing took place "at the door of the church, at the time of the Eucharist which they truly celebrated" (*Journal*, October 24, 1994). Thus we arrive at November 25, 1994. The bishops of Algeria wrote a message to their faithful flock in which they interpret the deeper meaning of all they are living through. With remarkable contemplative insight they stated that

> In the present crisis in Algeria more than at any other time, our Christian vocation shines in all its purity. It is an invitation to follow Christ along the road on which he makes his life into an offering for the people. In this offering God

expresses his tenderness for us all. We wish to live in Algeria God's covenant with all people, a covenant whose meaning the Bible has taught us throughout the history of salvation. We know that in this history God often used the faithful remnant of his people to save those who were to come afterwards. Such a vocation is common to all Christians wherever they may be, but our position as a minority in the midst of a Muslim people gives it a very special dimension. The people for whom we are called to consecrate our lives recognize Islam as a religious way that is different from ours. The offering of our lives passes over this barrier of different religious identities and bears witness to God's plan for the whole of humanity, which is to bring about communion among all mankind. It is this plan that Jesus wishes to preach when he announces that the kingdom of God is near. He sets it in motion by his life, death and resurrection. John writes that it was necessary "that Jesus should die for the nation, and not only for the nation, but to gather into one the dispersed children of God" (Jn 11:51) (*Letter from the Bishops of Algeria*, Tunis, November 25, 1994).

A month later, on December 27, four White Fathers (Missionaries of Africa) in Tizi Ouzou were assassinated: Jean Chevillar, Christian Cheissel, Alain Dieulangard and Charles Deckers, "immolated with the Friend whom they have followed beyond the call of duty," as Father Christopher would write in his *Journal*. Nine months later, on September 4, 1995, he wrote again:

At night, before the beginning of vigils, Christian announced that two of our sisters, Vivianne and Angela, had been assassinated this Sunday evening at Belcourt, coming out of Mass. I read and reread the Apocalypse. The reader must pay attention. Yes, it is you whom it is all about, Lamb slain yet conquering. It speaks of you, who are coming quickly. And I would like to be taken up in your movement of sacrificial life.

The next day Christopher continued:

> The announcement yesterday night continues to speak to me: "Revelation of Jesus Christ." It is a revelation from you: "Two of our sisters, Vivianne and Angela," said Christian, who had evidently not slept much. Yes, among our sisters there are two who are sisters in a more particular way, in crucified Love.

However, the wave of assassinations did not stop there. It continued to claim its many victims, among whom are some more religious. It would be Sister Odile Prévost who next gave the witness of her life, on November 10, 1995. Father Christopher tells us:

> At the end of terce, Christian announced the death of Sister Odile and Sister Chantal, Little Sisters of the Sacred Heart, who were assassinated in their own neighborhood. There is no other way for "the others" to become an offering sanctified by the Spirit and pleasing to God except by offering oneself in you, with you and through you. Chantal was only wounded (*Journal*, November 11, 1995, under the date of November 7, 1995).

A few days later, on November 21, the brothers of Atlas drew up a long detailed report to explain *How We Embody the Charism of our Order in the Present Situation*. In this valuable document, which is a sort of communal identity card, we read:

> After Christmas 1993, we all ratify our choice to live here together. This choice had been prepared by previous renunciations by each one of us (family, original community, country…). The violent death of one of us—or of all together—would simply be a consequence of this choice to live in the following of Christ (even if such a consequence was not directly foreseen in our constitutions!). Our bishop has often invited us by word and example to let ourselves be renewed like this, down to the very depths of the offering of our lives.

The Algerian bishops, who were both pastors and theologians, discovered the vocation of the Church in Algeria in the midst of the crisis which the country was going through. Our vocation, they said, consists in "an invitation to follow Christ along the road on which he makes his life into an offering for the people." The declaration of our brothers as a community finds its meaning in this living, contemplative context. There they say, "The violent death of one of us, or of all together, would simply be a consequence of this choice to live in the following of Christ." It was necessary that Jesus die for the nation, and not only for the nation, but also to gather into one the dispersed children of God! Whoever wants to serve me must follow me, and where I am, there also will my servants be.

2
A Revelation to the Youngest
How Far to Follow?

We can return to the chronology of blood and light begun in the preceding paragraphs. But now we do it from another perspective, that is, from the experience of the youngest of our witnesses. This "Christ-Bearer"—Christopher—is the one who, on the night before Christmas of 1993 when the group of armed guerrillas visited the monastery, escaped with an even younger brother and hid in the basement until vigils, fearing the worst. Several weeks later, he told Christian what he had experienced that night. What happened to me, he said, "was first like running away, then the hours of waiting, and finally like rising up from the abyss." He asked the Lord,

Where have you led me? Maybe you ask me to accept continuing my life, but can you ask me to accept the death of my brothers? (*Journal*, January 16, 1994).

Two weeks later he would write something else that refers to the incident:

A monk is nocturnal. How can I attain to intercession, vicarious representation and the prayer of supplication if I am still anxious about myself. In the darkness of the cellar last Christmas Eve you began to teach me this lesson when I believed that the others were in the hands of the visitors (*Journal*, February 4, 1994).

Similarly, when Christopher meditated on the community's experience of that Christmas Eve night, he wrote, "We are in a state of *epiclesis*" (*Relation*, January 4, 1994). He could not have said it better or more succinctly. The *epiclesis* of the Liturgy is the invocation of the Holy Spirit to come with his divine action and consecrate the gifts presented by the Church in the celebration of the Eucharist. Underneath Christopher's words we hear those of the second Eucharistic Prayer:

Let your Spirit come upon these gifts to make them holy, so that they may become for us the body and blood of our Lord, Jesus Christ.

The blood that is shed in following Jesus is found again in the Eucharist.

The *Journal* written by Christopher starting on August 8, 1993, is the best commentary on, and complement to, the *Testament* written by Christian. What the latter composed in a few weeks, Christopher wrote over the course of two and a half years. For one as for the other, it was a question of describing a plan of life faithfully followed to its ultimate consequences. This *Journal* has something special which sets it apart from previous diaries Christopher had written. There is a conscious effort to discern God's will and what God is saying, with a view to interpreting it and speaking from God's point of view. On one of its first pages he writes:

Already in this notebook, which is a feast-day gift,
    there is a presence; there is you.
And she also comes in.
    Oh, I am far from not being in it myself.
    I am far from forgetting myself
        in order to leave space for you,
    but I often write without looking at myself (too much).
I often write looking towards you.
Do you wish to teach me to write for you,
    for the service of your heart?
Am I inventing a mission for myself?
He who writes about the cross is a disciple. A child.
The world is waiting for the words of this childhood.
The Deceiver is lying in wait to devour these words,
    to pervert them as soon as they are born.
I will write in the desert.
I will defend your cause.
    If your breath takes my hand, I will obey your language.
Hearing you tell me to take up my cross
    makes me realize that, to do this,
I must leave what is occupying me
    (and preoccupying me): leave every other concern.
To follow you, totally lost in your own freedom
(*Journal*, August 1993).

In this context it is not surprising that Christopher—
knowing "that what we are, what is most precious in what
we are…has been given to us," asks himself, "The words in
this notebook, are they to be offered?" (*Journal*, August 23,
1993). Today, after knowing what happened, we can tell
Christopher with all certainty, "Yes, everything in your notebook was to be offered. You have not invented any mission
on your own. We know from Saint Benedict that God often
reveals what is best to the youngest (RB 3,3). It is precisely
you, the young revolutionary of May 1968—member of a
generation that is supposedly "incapable of commitment"!—
it is you who teach us by your journey from death to life
that life has meaning only when it is given away.

1993: Beginning a dangerous commitment

On August 22 the Catholic liturgy celebrates the Queenship of Mary. In the light of this liturgical commemoration, which was superseded that year by the Sunday celebration, Christopher felt moved to copy a text he had forgotten, but now found significant. Finding this text again made him wonder about its meaning for him now. The presence of the Woman is central. Our brother wrote:

> I recopy this scrap of writing found again yesterday among other papers. I had written:
> "Because of your body and blood, cries and tears, I have been able, I think, to be born.
> The way ahead is open.
> Very well. It only remains for me
> to follow
> at risk of you."
> Are these words true today?
> I live at risk of you.
> It is the Woman
> who is drawing me
> to this game (*Journal*, August 22, 1993).

That Sunday afternoon news of killings arrived that would crucify Christopher:

> Assassinations in Algiers. After so many others. This notebook cannot remain protected from such violence, which pierces through my whole being.

The next day, Monday the twenty-third, he still felt out of danger but, at the same time, invited by the Lord. He wrote:

> Yes. To be your body here exposes us to this violence which for the moment is not aimed at us. Wouldn't it be better if one man were to offer himself for this country? My servant, you say, will be where I am. I really have to follow you (*Journal*, August 23, 1993).

The community's retreat that year finished in the middle of December. Christopher ponders on his resolutions, fruits of his meditation and examination of conscience. He reflected:

> And so we have had our community retreat with Fr. Sanson. What remains of the points of the examen? Will there be some final decisive point for me to work on? Prayer? Yes, there is a point of adoration which you have placed at the end of a phase which I must live through, while moving without flinching towards that point....

> Yes, I have made the impossible resolution,
>   which I received from You.
> It is love that pushes me to it:
> This is my body: given.
> This is my blood: shed.
> Let it be done to me according to your word;
>   may your action pierce my whole being.
> And this resolution—which is yours
>   —goes infinitely beyond me.
> Near the Woman (You, the Son born of her flesh,
>   authorize me to call her "Mama" and to take her to
>   my home), my resolution is quite simple: I am.
> A resolution stronger than death
> (*Journal*, December 22, 1993).

Ahead, the path toward the gift of himself was open. It passed through the Eucharist and through the Mother of Jesus. When he gave his consent, Christopher made his own the words of Mary: "Let it be done to me according to your word."

A few days later, on December 31, the anniversary of his first profession, Christopher remembered the homily the superior gave on that occasion. In the Islamic calendar it was the day of *Achoura*—from the Arabic, *achra*, "ten"; *achoura* being the tenth day of the month *Moharram*—a day specially consecrated to almsgiving on which the wealthy are invited to give a tenth of their profits to the poor. Christian wanted

Atlas to give ten percent of its annual honey harvest to the poorest and most needy of their neighbors. In his homily at the profession ceremony, the superior at the time, Father John Baptist, asked Christopher's father and mother, who were present, to offer one of their twelve children. "Profession," he said, "is the gift of oneself to God. As the verse which the young monk sings puts it, 'Receive me, O Lord, according to your word and I shall live' [Ps 119:116 and RB 58,21]. This self-gift only ends the day of our death." That is why Christopher would write:

> On that day of *Achoura*, December 31, 1976,
>   Fr. John Baptist had spoken
> of the offering of 1/12 of my brs. and srs.
>   Then he spoke of your hand.
> Also of the day of death as the true profession.
> In your hands, Mary,
> in your hands, Church in Algeria,
> I give myself to crucified Love
> that he may profess me
> as his well-beloved,
> consecrated in your
> I am
> the Way, Truth, Life.

These words of self-gift, through the mediation of both Mary and the Church in Algeria, are better understood if we remember that a few days before, on Christmas Eve, the community had received the visit of the GIA group commanded by Sayat-Attya. The armed guerillas made a particularly strong impression due to the fact that two weeks before the same group had assassinated twelve Croats who lived near the monastery. Moreover, the very day the above words were written, December 31, the community had taken a series of votes which revealed a strong consensus in favor of staying where they were.

1994: A Request for Help and the Search for Meaning

Blessed Maria Gabriella Sagheddu is well known in the world of ecumenism, especially in Trappist monasteries. Pope John Paul II has proposed her as a model of spiritual ecumenism because of the gift of her own life for the cause of unity among Christians (*Ut unum sint*, 27). We celebrate her feast day on April 22. On that day Christopher remembered her affectionately, addressed her in Italian and asked her, with fear and trepidation, for her hand:

> Maria Gabriella, Mia Sorella, dare I ask for your...hand to help me? You succeeded in giving your life. Will I manage to do so, today? (*Journal*, April 22, 1994).

Throughout 1994 eight religious and priests fell victims of violent deaths. Christopher did not forget them:

> Paule-Hélene, Henri, Esther, Caridad, Alain, Jean,
>   Charlie, Christian;
> they are all alive in your words, "I am"
> (*Journal*, December 28, 1994).

In particular, the death of four White Fathers on December 27 made Christopher think about martyrdom. The subject had already been raised in the community dialogues. On July 17 Christian had written a meditation in memory of the first African martyrs, but the chief message concerned the Algerian martyrs of today. The latter were called "*Hidden witnesses of a hope.*" Christopher's reflections centered on Thomas Becket, Archbishop of Canterbury, assassinated on December 29, 1170, for his fidelity to the Church. It seems that Christopher had recently read T. S. Eliot's *Murder in the Cathedral*, with its psychological and theological analysis of what it means to be a martyr. He now made his own the words the playwright put into the mouth of Thomas during the latter's final Christmas homily in Canterbury Cathedral four days before his death. Thomas, and Christopher with him, speak to us:

A Christian martyrdom is no accident. Still less is a Christian martyrdom the result of a man's will to become a martyr, as a man by willing and contriving may become a ruler of men. A martyrdom is never the design of man; for the true martyr is he who has become the instrument of God, who has lost his will in the will of God, not lost it but found it, for he has found freedom in submission to God. The martyr no longer desires anything for himself, not even the glory of martyrdom (*Journal*, December 28, 1994).

There was something, however, that preoccupied Christopher even more. Apparently the GIA's plan against the White Fathers was not simply to assassinate them. They had thought of taking them hostage, which is precisely what would happen later to the seven monks of Atlas. From the perspective of faith, Christopher looked for a reply to the question troubling him:

Will you [Christian Cheissel] tell me if their true intention—stained with murderous madness—was to take you as hostages? I would like to know. I am thinking about it because of how this process might continue…in Algiers? …at Tibhirine? A hostage takes the place of others, but it must be a free commitment on his part, in order that this role of victim be filled with love and forgiveness. Jesus alone can draw us there, giving us a share in his role of being the Son who is infinitely Brother…. As a friend of yours, I have to pray for your assassins (*Journal*, January 4, 1995).

The conclusion here may strike us as surprising. It is that the only way to become a Christian hostage some day is to pray for one's enemies.

1995: Asking for an Immense Grace

On July 25 the Church traditionally celebrates the feast of Saint Christopher, a martyred Roman soldier decapitated in Lycia during the persecution under the Emperor Decius.

July 25 is also the feast of Saint James, son of Zebedee and brother of John the Evangelist. An ancient tradition associates him with the Christian victory over the Moslems in the battle of Clavijo, Spain, in 834. Ever since the eleventh century pilgrims from all over Europe come to his shrine at Santiago de Compostela to venerate this "Soldier of Christ." Father Chistopher, however, writing in 1995, put this context of war and victory over the Moslems totally to one side when he asked for a special grace, precisely on this feast of his own saint. It was that he be identified with Jesus, the suffering servant and son of man who gives his life as a ransom for all...in Moslem territory (cf. Mk 10:45 and Is 53:11).

> I ask you on this day for the grace to become a servant
>   and to give my life
>   here
>   as a ransom for peace
>   as a ransom for life
>   Jesus draw me
>   into your joy
>   of crucified love (*Journal*, July 25, 1995).

We should not think that the servant giving his "life here as a ransom for peace" considers himself greater or better than others. On the contrary. Christmas time, when God becomes a child, is a good moment to learn the lesson of being small so as to become great. It is this conviction that made Christopher write the way he did a few days before Christmas:

> Since merely a yes
> is enough for you
> to do the impossible here
> take me, please
>   (*Journal*, December 21, 1995).

1996: A Marian Gift of Self

Christmas 1995 arrived. Christopher had made a crêche out of the *cashabia* (a camel-hair tunic with a large hood) of Henri Vergès, who had been assassinated the previous year. Christopher turned the hood into a cave, in which he put the little statues of the Holy Family. The symbolism was both eloquent and heart-rending. Christopher comments on it in his diary:

> Behold the lamb. He is here. Soon comes the marriage.
> In the folds of a *cashabia*—stronger than murder
>   —it is he, born in the midst of us
> to be offered
> in our lives (*Journal*, Jan. 16 1996).

The new life of this Child is stronger than any assassination and death. Very soon there would be shouts of joy and victory in heaven at the wedding feast of the Lamb (Rev 19:1-10). There was, however, still a path to climb. So the question which Isaac the Patriarch and Christopher the Monk ask as they climb Mount Moria is a good one (Gen 22:7): "Where is the lamb for the hill of sacrifice?" (*Journal*, January 17, 1996). It is still the time for struggle:

> The lamb and the dove above it are coming to set me free from the beasts struggling within me for my life (*Journal*, January 18, 1996)

Toward the end of January Christopher asked permission for a prophetic gesture. It was Sunday the twenty-eighth, the Lord's Day. He was speaking with his prior about the priesthood. Five years had passed since his own ordination to the priesthood.

> I expressed a desire to Christian, whom I talked with this morning: "No stole should go over my cowl if I die, because the sign will have given way to the reality." It remains for me to allow the Holy Spirit to accomplish it

and to make me a newly ordained priest of Algeria (*Journal*, January 28, 1996).

He was looking for the reality beyond the signs. He had to be open to the action of the Spirit, so that the Spirit can bring to completion the anointing that took place at the time of ordination. It is the only way that the victim will be totally transformed into another Christ, another anointed one, another messiah. The priestly offering had been in a state of *epiclesis* now for over two years. Three weeks later there was another prophetic gesture, this time not asked for but ready-made. The context of violence brought it forth and was its context. Not much time remained. Everything was almost ready:

> Violence and bloodshed in the country again and again. I planted my second cross somewhere in the garden. Sister M-E made it and gave it to me. It is a Franciscan cross in the form of a T. I have put back round my neck the one made by Bernard [of Dombes]. When will the time come to be planted at Tibhirine: planted in you, my Beloved? (*Journal*, February 19, 1996).

He was not trying to anticipate his burial so much as his being scattered as seed. If the grain of wheat does not fall to the earth and die it bears no fruit, but if it dies it bears much fruit.

March 19 arrives, the Solemnity of Saint Joseph, husband of Mary and patron of the universal Church. It is a day with strong Marian overtones that need to be brought into the open. It was the right moment to become an "offering."

> Today is the anniversary of my consecration to Mary. Yes, I continue to choose you, Mary, with Joseph, in the communion of all the saints—and I receive you from the hands of Jesus with the poor and the sinners. Like the beloved disciple, I take you into my home. Near you, I am what I should be: offered.

Glad to be "offered," Christopher adds, "I was happy to preside at the Eucharist." And then,

It was as if I heard the voice of Joseph inviting me to sing Psalm 100 with him and the child: "My song is of mercy and justice.... I will walk in the way of perfection. O when, Lord, will you come? I will walk with blameless heart" (*Journal*, March 19, 1996).

This is the finale of the sung symphony: Jesus, Joseph and Christopher singing in a trio, "I will walk with blameless heart." They are the last words of the *Journal*.

Christopher's reflections prove beyond a shadow of a doubt that his *Journal* completes and points to his prior's last *Testament*. The *Journal*—this clear, bubbling stream of gentle water flowing from the faithful, generous, poetic heart of a French revolutionary of May 1968—is a moving picture of growth toward the final act of giving one's own life. It is this same gift of self that we see captured in a flash of peaceful light, in all its radiant maturity, in Christian's *Testament*. Both works, the more concise one of the prior and the longer one of the novice master, flow from a common reservoir of convictions shared by their whole community, which in no way takes away from their intensely personal quality. Both *Testament* and *Journal* are now treasured portions of our spiritual patrimony. Together, they show how the key to understanding the glorious passion of the brothers of Atlas lies in the gift of one's own life for Christ and his gospel.

3
Too Big a Heritage
Coheirs with the Church in Algeria

The small, suffering, eloquent Church in Algeria is faced with a frightening challenge. Many expect her to witness to the total following of the gospel, even to the shedding of martyrs' blood. Christians and Moslems, believers and non-

believers, have our eyes on this Church in Algeria, waiting
for a dramatic gesture of hope in the midst of this broken
world in which we live. Such an expectation goes beyond
what human strength can do, though nothing is impossible
for God.

This Church in Algeria is the true place where the memory
of our brothers is to be kept alive. She is the heir to the patrimony of our martyrs, which is too big for us to receive
alone. We want to be in solidarity with her, so that we can
be true coheirs. But to be coheirs with this Church of martyrs we have to be completely open to monastic martyrdom,
totally committed to a long life full of little pinpricks, shedding our blood in the patient passion of daily living.

Today, as on the day of our profession, we are called to
say, "Receive me, Lord, according to your word and I shall
live; do not disappoint me in my hope!" Our vow of
conversatio morum can be understood as a promise to follow
Jesus in the monastic life. The way of obedience-silence-
humility (RB 5-7), of good zeal and good works (RB 72 and
4), is our monastic way of following him. This is how we
move toward the Lord and give ourselves to him so as to be
completely transformed into him. In fact this is the only way
that we can be witnesses and coheirs with the Church of
martyrs that suffers and rejoices in Algeria. We know our
own weakness, but let us pray confidently with Bernard of
Clairvaux that there be a change:

> "Draw me after you; we shall run in the odor of your oint-
> ment." It is indeed necessary that we be drawn, Lord,
> because the fire of your love has quickly cooled within
> us. We cannot run now as we did in former days, because
> of this coldness that freezes the waters of grace. But we
> shall run again when you restore to us the joy of knowing
> that you are our Savior: when the benign warmth of grace
> returns with the new shining of the Sun of Justice. The
> troubles that darken the sky like thunderclouds will then
> pass away. The soft breath of the caressing breeze will

melt the frozen ointments and the perfumes will rise to fill the air with their sweetness. Then we shall run: run with eagerness where the fragrances draw us. The lethargy that now weighs us down will vanish with the return of fervor. We will no longer need to be drawn. We will be spurred on by the perfumes and run of our own accord. But meanwhile, until then, "Draw me after you" (SC 21:4).

There is still more. Communiqués 43 and 44 from the GIA (of April 18 and May 22, 1996) make it clear that our seven brothers were executed for being monks and Christians. We, too, are monks and Christians. Because of this we have a debt of forgiveness which we owe the GIA. We owe it, above all, to Abou Abdel Rahmân Amîn, more commonly known as Djamel Zitouni, the head of the Armed Islamic Group and the person responsible for sentencing and beheading our brothers.

However, it is not just a debt of forgiveness that we owe to this last-minute friend. We also want to make a covenant with him, a covenant of fraternal communion. The mass media informed us on July 16, 1996, that Djamel Zitouni had died, a victim of the violence in which he had lived and believed. Djamel and Christian, please God, have met again in Paradise as two blessed thieves. Both one and the other, together with the other six, are our brothers forever. To all eight of them we want to say THANK YOU and A-DIEU. We see you in the face of God. And this heritage is too big for us because it is without measure. But nothing is impossible for God!

Bernardo Olivera
Abbot General

CHAPTER V
Messages Received

1
Letter from the Secretariat of State
(about the Testament of Father Christian)

SECRETARIAT OF STATE   Vatican City, June 4, 1996

N. 390.451

Dear Reverend Father,

I am pleased to inform you that the Holy Father thanks you most cordially for your thoughtfulness in sending him the "spiritual testament" of Father Christian Marie de Chergé, prior of the Atlas monastery, whose dramatic death was confirmed a few days ago, as was that of the six other brothers from that community.

His Holiness, who has closely followed the recent events from the moment of the abduction of these Trappist brothers and has kept them very much in his prayers, now prays that the Lord may reward their generous sacrifice. At the same time, he is deeply moved and strengthened by Father Christian's "spiritual testament," in which is so evident the greatness of soul with which these brothers lived through such particularly hostile situations. What is especially striking is their total availability to give up their lives completely, with words of reconciliation and gratitude in perfect conformity to Christ crucified.

The Holy Father wishes to express again his hope that the blood shed by this community of monks be a seed of concord in the nation which they loved and for which they gave their lives. He invites the Trappist family to thank the Lord for the gift of the life and death of these brothers by praying for them and continuing the prayer which the brothers began. With these sentiments of appreciation, and as an expression of his particular affection for the Trappist brothers and sisters, he gives them wholeheartedly his Apostolic Blessing.

Uniting myself, also, to the prayers for these religious brothers, I take advantage of this opportunity to assure you of my personal esteem in Christ.

> \+ G. B. Re
> Substitute

Rev. Fr. Bernardo Olivera
Abbot General of the Cistercian Order
    of the Strict Observance
ROME

2
Testament of Father Christian
(opened on Pentecost Sunday, May 26, 1996)

When we face an A-DIEU...
If it should happen one day—and it could be today—
that I become a victim of the terrorism
    which now seems ready to engulf
all the foreigners living in Algeria,
I would like my community, my Church and my family
to remember that my life was GIVEN
    to God and to this country.
I ask them to accept the fact
    that the One Master of all life
was not a stranger to this brutal departure.
I would ask them to pray for me:
for how could I be found worthy of such an offering?
I ask them to associate this death
    with so many other equally violent ones
which are forgotten through indifference or anonymity.
My life has no more value than any other.
Nor any less value.
In any case, it has not the innocence of childhood.
I have lived long enough to know
    that I am an accomplice in the evil
which seems, alas, to prevail in the world,
even in the evil which might blindly strike me down.
I would like, when the time comes,
    to have a moment of spiritual clarity
which would allow me to beg forgiveness of God
and of my fellow human beings,
and at the same time forgive with all my heart
    the one who will strike me down.
        I could not desire such a death.

It seems to me important to state this.
I do not see, in fact, how I could rejoice
if the people I love were indiscriminately
    accused of my murder.
It would be too high a price to pay
    for what will perhaps be called
    the "grace of martyrdom"
to owe this to an Algerian, whoever he may be,
especially if he says he is acting in fidelity
    to what he believes to be Islam.
I am aware of the scorn which can be heaped
    on the Algerians indiscriminately.
I am also aware of the caricatures of Islam
    which a certain Islamism fosters.
It is too easy to soothe one's conscience
by identifying this religious way with
    the fundamentalist ideology of its extremists.
For me, Algeria and Islam are not that,
    but rather a body and a soul.
I have proclaimed this often enough, I think,
    in the light of what I have received from it.
I so often find there that true strand of the Gospel
    which I learned at my mother's knee,
    my very first Church,
precisely in Algeria, and already inspired
    with respect for Muslim believers.
Obviously, my death will appear to confirm
those who hastily judged me naive or idealistic:
"Let him tell us now what he thinks of it!"
But these persons should know that finally
    my most avid curiosity will be set free.
This is what I shall be able to do, please God:
immerse my gaze in that of the Father
to contemplate with him His children of Islam
just as he sees them, all shining with the glory of Christ,
the fruit of His Passion, filled with the Gift of the Spirit

whose secret joy will always be to establish communion
and restore the likeness, playing with the differences.
    For this life lost, totally mine and totally theirs,
I thank God, who seems to have willed it entirely
    for the sake of that JOY in everything
    and in spite of everything.
In this THANK YOU, which is said
    for everything in my life from now on,
I certainly include you, friends of yesterday and today,
and you, my friends of this place,
along with my mother and father,
    my sisters and brothers and their families.
You are the hundredfold granted as was promised!
And also you, my last-minute friend,
    who will not have known what you were doing:
Yes, I want this THANK YOU and this "A-DIEU"
    to be for you, too,
because in God's face I see yours.
May we meet again as happy thieves
in Paradise, if it please God, the Father of us both.
                   AMEN! IN H'ALLAH!

              Algiers, December 1, 1993
              Tibhirine, January 1, 1994
                     Christian+

3
Message of John Paul II
to the Brothers and Sisters Meeting at Tre Fontane
(on the Occasion of a Memorial Mass
for the Martyrs of Atlas)

Very Dear Brothers and Sisters,

With a keen sense of participation, I unite with you as you gather around the altar to celebrate, in the sacrifice of Christ, the memory of your seven confreres of the monastery of Our Lady of Atlas, at Tibhirine, in Algeria, who were killed in a barbaric manner last May. With this message I wish to express my spiritual nearness to you and my solidarity, along with a special remembrance in my prayers.

"Unless a grain of wheat falls to the ground and dies, it remains just a grain of wheat; but if it dies, it produces much fruit. Whoever loves his life loses it, and whoever hates his life in this world will preserve it for eternal life. Whoever serves me must follow me, and where I am, there also will my servant be. The Father will honor whoever serves me" (John 12:24-26).

How pertinent these words of the gospel are! How appropriate they sound, as we think of your seven confreres and of your present capitular meetings which are taking place in the light of their testimony! The Lord alone can comfort his children in such dramatic trials. Faith in Christ, crucified and risen, tears aware the veil of suffering and makes us understand the mysterious fecundity of the death of believers, whose life is not taken away but transformed.

I am certain that the sacrifice of the monks of Tibhirine has not failed to provide special inspiration for your capitular labors, enabling each of you to meet with full openness of Spirit the two great challenges which face you: that of a renewed fidelity to the radical following of Christ, and that of communion within the great Cistercian family. Be certain of this: the blood of martyrs is in the Church a force for renewal and of unity.

"At the end of the second millennium, the Church has become once again a Church of martyrs" (*Tertio millennio adveniente*, n. 37). The testimony of the Trappists of Our Lady of Atlas takes its place alongside that of the Bishop of Oran, His Excellency Pierre Lucien Caverie, and of not a few other sons and daughters on the African continent who, during this period, have given their lives for the Lord and for their brothers and sisters, beginning with those who persecuted and killed them. Their witness is the victory of the Cross, the victory of the merciful love of God, who saves the world. The testament which Dom Christian de Chergé left behind, offered to all the key for understanding the tragic occurrence in which he and his confreres were involved, the final meaning of which is the gift of one's life in Christ. "My life," he wrote, "was given to God and to this country."

Venerable Brothers and Sisters, you are the custodians of this memory, guardians in prayer, in common discernment, and in the concrete directives which you decide upon, so that the memory of this event be fruitful in the future for Trappists and for the whole Church. In this rich promise of hope, we invoke the abundance of the gifts of the Holy Spirit on each of you and on the works of your respective Chapters, and we impart to you with all our heart the Apostolic Benediction.

From the "A. Gemelli" Hospital,
October 10, 1996
John Paul II